DARE TO BE A DIFFERENCE *Maker*

Volume 3

Margie,
Welcome to CareerFusion!
Glad to have met you!

Hugs,
[illegible]

DARE TO BE A DIFFERENCE *Maker*

Volume 3

DIFFERENCE MAKERS WHO DARE TO LIVE
WITH PASSION, FOLLOW THEIR PURPOSE
AND COMMIT TO HELPING OTHERS!

MICHELLE PRINCE

Performance Publishing Group
McKinney, TX

ISBN-10:0984754741
ISBN-13:978-0-9847547-4-8

www.DareToBeADifferenceMaker.com

Dedication

To all the "Difference Makers" in the world who are making a difference by following your heart.
Thank you for letting your "light" shine!

Introduction

For many years, as I worked in "Corporate America", I would say to myself, *"I just want to make a difference!"* I was selling software and I'm sure I was making some difference for my clients but not in the way I wanted to. I wanted to help, serve, encourage and motivate people. I wanted to make a positive impact on their lives but I didn't know how…how could just one person really make a significant difference? So, I didn't…for a long time. I continued to work in an area that wasn't my passion or calling. I didn't follow my heart and God's promptings to go in the direction of my purpose and dreams. Instead, I just let year after year go by feel unfulfilled, unhappy and spiritually broken.

That is, until one day in 2008 when I had my "aha" moment. It hit me like a ton of bricks that it's my responsibility to follow my passions and purpose. No one can do that for me. I took action to write my first book, Winning In Life Now, began to speak, motivate and mentor others to live their best life and, as they say, "the rest is history."

What I found over this journey is that we all have a desire to make a difference. We all want to live with passion and follow our God-given callings; our purpose. It's through this understanding that I decided to write this series of books.

Dare To Be A Difference Maker 3, is my vision to have a unique collection of narratives, not only from inspired leaders, but also from those I see making a difference and impacting others in their everyday personal and professional life. These stories are about real people who are making a real difference even on a small scale.

My mission in creating the **"Difference Maker Movement"** and in writing the series of *Dare To Be A Difference Maker* books is that you will gain inspiration, wisdom & the courage you need in order to get through life's tough challenges and make a difference for others in the process.

So many people I speak with these days discuss their issues as though they are losing hope. It is my vision for this book to reach the masses and have a powerful effect on people in their everyday lives. It is my prayer that this book, and all the volumes, will breathe new life into your mind and spirit and that it will inspire you to take action in order to help others.

I've selected an exclusive group of difference-makers who I know can motivate, inspire and be a part of a movement to change people's lives. Everyone can do this; it just takes commitment and honoring of our unique and sacred gifts. It is to those people, I dedicate this book.

From one "Difference Maker" to another,

Michelle

P.S. Do you or anyone you know, have a story about making a difference? We are currently interviewing authors for our next book and would love to have you join us in this amazing journey. To submit an entry, please contact Info@PrincePerformance.com for more details. While one powerful story can be fascinating, many can move mountains!

Table of Contents

1

When "Why" Asks "Why?"

Kim Warren Martin

"To be yourself in a world that is constantly trying to make you something else is the greatest accomplishment."

--Ralph Waldo Emerson

In July 2013, I walked away from a 27-year career in the technology industry. It was scary, uncomfortable, I thought people would think I was crazy…and yet it was liberating. That was the day I started to make a difference for me.

The Beginning

As a child, I believed that my very presence on earth was such a unique expression of God's creative abilities that it was my sworn duty to be ALL He created me to be. And by doing that, I would bring glory to Him, positively impact lives and leave the world a better place. I didn't know how I was going to do this, but that was my dream.

I grew to love the arts and wanted to be involved in anything creative. I loved acting. I was even certain that I'd be the first African-American woman to win an Oscar. However, since I was number one of four girls and my parents wanted to make certain we were able to "take care of ourselves," at the age of 18, I entered engineering school instead of performing arts school. No amount of respectful objecting could seem to convince them that going to engineering school was not the best path to Hollywood. So off I went. At the age of 21 I graduated from engineering school and started my career in the technology industry, which appeared to overturn my childhood dream and obviously cleared the way for Halle Berry to take home my Oscar.

Studying engineering wasn't all bad because while I didn't see engineering as artsy, I learned that engineers are remarkably creative. And even in the technology industry creative opportunities found their way to me. One such opportunity came on my first job when I was asked to make training videos to help customers understand how to use the company's pharmaceutical software. Making those videos was exciting and helped me to see that creativity could happen outside of Hollywood.

Over the years as I worked at settling into my career, visions of Hollywood became a distant memory. I enjoyed the salary, travel, flexibility and other perks that came with my roles in Corporate America. Six years into working for my last employer, I accepted a position where I focused on helping women to advance in their careers. It was deeply rewarding to see people grow and reach their career goals yet on some level, the more I helped others the more I felt misplaced. And periodically I would feel something inside me gasp as if it were taking its last breath.

One day instead of a gasp, I heard the question "Why?" in my gut. And in an instant, I knew that the previous gasps were my why struggling to gather up enough strength to ask me "Why?" Why was I so dedicated to helping everyone else go for their dreams and so irresponsible with my own? As blessed as I felt helping others, it became clear that no one, not even me, was looking out for my *why*. And after nearly 30 years it was time for me to take responsibility for MY dream and making a difference in my OWN life.

The Question

When my why started asking me "why?", it literally unnerved

me. Instead of going along with the fact that I had stopped dreaming and perfected listening to the voice of reason, my why was challenging me to once again find the path to fulfilling the sworn duty I'd felt as a child to be ALL God created me to be. Although I'd put energy into planning many of my own career moves, what I'd really done was discounted my dream and moved from job to job building other people's dreams. I let one of my own deepest needs go unmet for nearly three decades. It brought me to tears because deep down inside I knew no matter how many explanations I entertained, I didn't have an answer worthy of the question and I felt like it might be too late.

Some people seem to come into the world not only knowing their destiny, but getting on the path to achieving it very early in life. Sadly most of us don't. We ignore our inner yearnings and callings. We are directed to trade them in for the comforts of societal and familial norms. Go to college, get a job, get married, buy a house, have a family, be responsible, take care of your family and show your children how to do the same. While these are all good things, often they don't encourage, or allow, us to be ALL we were created to be. It takes courage, conviction and commitment to buck the norm. And that question showed me that I had played it safe far too long.

Even though my creative talents and abilities found a way to invade the scenes throughout my career. However, that wasn't enough. I wasn't discounting my career successes, but when I broadened my definition and rated my success relative to my dusty dreams, it was a big letdown. Some people call this being responsible and "doing what you have to do". I get that. Believe me. But, life is not a dress rehearsal. My dream was dying and I had a conscious choice to make: revive it or potentially say good-bye to it forever.

The Decision

So "why?" became "how?" I wasn't exactly sure what would be the vehicle, but I was open and excited about becoming ALL I was created to be. A short time later I was introduced to a life-changing opportunity and became an independent distributor in a ground-floor health and wellness company, which I immediately jumped on, but it took me TWO AND A HALF YEARS to make the leap from employee to entrepreneur. During that time I agonized over when I would actually make my move. I continued to give power to fear and the voice of fear kept telling me that I was ruining my life. Reason told me that people would think I was crazy for leaving the job I had and the company I worked for…especially during these economic times. When I would listen to my why, it would tell me the exact opposite. That everything I needed was already inside me. That my career was a stepping stone, not a destination. Fear harassed me with questions like "Who in the world do you think YOU are expecting more? You should be glad that you made it this far!" Reason said that I should hang on to my job until I could get full retirement benefits. After all it was only 12 more years. My why said "Don't procrastinate. The best time to follow your dream is now" So who had the more solid case?

I found myself uncomfortable with the thought of walking away from my job and steady paycheck, but the thought of staying was equally unsettling. I discussed it with my husband over and over again until he was almost as weary as I was. Not only did I feel completely out of my comfort zone and scared out of my wits, but now I was dragging my husband onto my emotional roller coaster—he wasn't enjoying the ride. He is a peacemaker and loves peace, so I needed to stop making him crazy.

Shortly thereafter, I let my manager know that I planned to quit and focus on our wellness business. While voicing my decision was a great relief, it also granted fear and reason the opportunity to sow additional seeds of doubt. But at this point, I'd resolved not to turn back and was no longer fertile ground for their bad seeds. For the first few days, I thought many times about telling my manager that I was just kidding and didn't really plan to leave my job. But I resisted the urge to let those words even come out jokingly. Surprisingly, on my last day I felt a sense of peace, release and excitement.

Later I learned that instead of thinking I was insane and ruining my life, many of my colleagues saw me as bold, daring, courageous and gutsy. A previous manager even said they would love to do the same thing but just didn't have the courage. Wow!

The Process

My identity was tightly coupled with my career, so leaving it was not easy. Who was I apart from my job title? Emerson's quote is spot on. It's easy to fall in line and follow the crowd, but it takes courage to follow the road less traveled. My hope is to inspire people who want to give life to their dying dreams. I quit my job to give myself the space to think and be creative, but you may not need to. You may be led to do something innovative or creative right where you are. Only you can determine that. But I'd like to briefly share a few tips that I found helpful in making my decision:

1. Start by getting in touch with your WHY. In his book *Put Your Dream to the Test,* John Maxwell says that a key step is to answer the ownership question—Is your dream really YOUR dream? My career was not really MY dream. I found ways to relate it to my dream, but it wasn't exactly my dream. If your dream is really YOUR dream, own it and decide to do everything you can to achieve it. The *how* will come.
2. Get in touch with WHO you really are. I believe what you do should be a reflection of who you are. My dream is to use my creative abilities to help others clear a path to their purpose and why. That's who I am and I OWN that When I took that last position on my job, my work started to reflect who I am. When we started our health and wellness business, it was even more of a reflection of who I am.

   Who are you? Imagine yourself being the absolute best YOU possible. Spend time alone writing down details about how it feels when you are at your best—extreme details—where you want to live, who you want to be with, how you want to spend your days, what you want to wear, how you want to feel physically and mentally, how much money you want to have, what charities do you want to support and what legacy do you want to leave. Give yourself permission to dream…BIG. Operate out of your imagination, not your memory. Don't let your past hold you back. Forget others' opinions. Don't let your age or bank account impose unnecessary restrictions on your identifying your best life. Recently in his sermon entitled *Divine Expectations*, Bishop TD Jakes said "be fruitful and multiply from where you are". As long as there is breath in your body you can begin to give life to your dream.

3. Recognize HOW important of a role your own belief/mindset and commitment play in achieving your dream. I've heard it said that your actions will always follow your beliefs. Our beliefs can stop us or propel us forward. In the past I wouldn't allow my beliefs to go in the direction of my dream. I was most comfortable letting them go in the direction of my job. When my why asked why, I grabbed hold of MY dream. Belief in MY dream has brought about changes in my thinking, expectations and I've learned that I don't need others' approval to move forward. If you are married, you may need to get agreement from your spouse. But that doesn't mean he/she will share your vision or join you. It's easier when you have supporters and cheerleaders, but you don't need them. Understand that the journey may be a lonely one, but you can make it. Resolve not to quit. Eric Thomas said "The pain of achieving your dream is temporary and will eventually subside, but if you quit it will last forever."
4. Decide WHEN you want to be your best. You have to put an end date in place. Don't be afraid to be aggressive. Don't let yourself off the hook. Find accountability partner(s) to help keep you on task. Put dates on major milestones and share them with others who can hold you accountable to meeting them. Make a dream board and study it every day.

5. Realize that WHAT you do daily will either help or hinder your progress. Productivity requires discipline and organization. For some odd reason, this one is a big challenge for me right now. Managing projects on my job was easier because someone else set the goals and objectives for the company and I did my part to help achieve them. Now I am that someone. I am the CEO of my business and own the vision, mission and projects. Now that I have time to think and be creative, I have so many ideas running through my head that I'm sometimes challenged to set clear priorities.

   There are many systems out there to help you get organized. I encourage you to look for one that resonates with you. Michelle Prince's *Busy Being Busy* is a great place to start. Whatever you choose, set clear priorities, organize your time, be excellent at follow up and make sure that each day includes time for personal development and reflection.

The Future

As women we often put others' needs ahead of our own. If you want to make a difference in your own life I suggest that you start to put your own mask on first. Then you can bring others along. This is not a license to neglect your relationships and responsibilities, but permission to look at how you might change some of what you're doing to create space for you…your dream. It is a suggestion to help you serve others even better by serving yourself first. Jim Rohn said that the greatest gift you can give to somebody is your own personal development. "I will take care of me for you if you will take care of you for me."

Today I am creating a new and different life for myself, and making an even greater difference in the lives of others. I now get to show the world what I'm really made of…why I'm really here. And I LOVE IT!!!

Martin Luther King, Jr. said, "Faith is taking the first step even when you don't see the whole staircase." If your why is asking you why, you now have a decision to make. Like mine, it may not be an easy one, but it will be worth it. ■

Kim Warren Martin

Kim Warren Martin is an illustrative speaker, best-selling author and transformative wellness and wealth strategist. She is committed to helping people clear a path to purpose through wellness. As an outcome of her personal pursuit of wellness, she has helped transform lives through forming healthy living habits and establishing healthy monetary patterns.

Recently leaving a 20+ year career in the technology industry, she concentrates on helping provide wellness through the Kyani opportunity. She is a proud member of Delta Sigma Theta Sorority, Inc., listed in Who's Who Among Executives and Professionals and a recent affiliate of the National Association of Professional Women. Read her blog at kimwarrenmartin.com.

twitter: @KimWarrenMartin
Linked In: Kim Warren Martin

2

One Moment Can Change Your Life Forever

By Bob Johnson

Birth, a kiss, marriage, divorce, death, a gun-shot, a car or plane crash can change your life forever. I will always remember September 11, 2001, where in a moment planes crashed into the Twin Towers killing thousands of unsuspecting Americans as well as over 400 first responders who died in their valiant rescue efforts. The families of all those who died on that fateful day will never be the same. I know that there are pivotal moments that have changed your life; hopefully, for the good but that's not always the case. I remember in my own life when I was just a baby, a plane crashed in WW II and in a moment, my father's life ended and the little baby, Robert J. McWilliams, Jr.'s life would never be the same. War would claim my father, adoption would later change my name but my father's honor and valor are my inheritance until the day I die and I know that we will meet again someday.

Regardless of Circumstances You Must Make the Best of Your Life

That is true, but I was just a baby when my father died and I had no control over what would happen. I was living in an oil camp two miles from Luling, Texas with my grandparents while my mother searched for a new life. However, these were the happiest times of my childhood (ages one-seven) and the memory of my grand-parents and their love and care for me still lingers 70 years later.

The things in your memory are about the only thing that you can take with you when you leave this good earth and love is the best friend you can take on your new journey. Those were good years, filled with great memories but in a moment my life would change forever. My mother with her new husband returned and off we would go to another oil camp on the King Ranch near the Mexican border. Bitter tears filled my eyes as I was torn (I didn't want to go) from the loving arms of my grandparents and thrust into the care of strangers that I had never seen before. I was carried off to a place I had never been before. Looking back, it's admirable that a mother, regardless of past circumstances, would want to take care of her child and a man who had never laid eyes on me would assume the responsibilities of raising me and adopting me as his son. However, at the time, it seemed like an abrupt ending to the only loving and caring relationship I had ever known and the next four years would be difficult.

The "Make Believe" World of Danielle Steele Would Be Easier to Write About

That is true, because the pain of the next four years made it difficult to even remember much of what happened from ages seven to ten. I am sure there were some good times, but here is about all I remember. I remember that the King Ranch was a remote desolate place with mesquite trees, cactus and rattlesnakes. At night in my little room, I remember feeling sad and alone with no one to turn to. I remember crying my eyes out when my little baby rabbit that I had found and placed in a shoe box in my room was killed by a rat that had come through a crack in the floor. I remember being slapped for calling my step father "Bill" instead of dad. Most memorable was the little school which was 95% Mexican with mostly Spanish spoken in the classroom. You can guess it: I didn't understand or speak Spanish and for four years, my education was limited to say the least. Writing seems to be good therapy where you can express feelings that you have always had, but maybe, felt embarrassed or afraid to share your story with your country club friends. My story of growing up in poverty in the oil fields of South Texas with limited education lives within me and motivates me to help other people, especially kids who need a helping hand.

Thank God, All Things Change

In another moment in time, my step father was transferred to a new oil camp near Charlotte, Texas south of San Antonio. Compared to the King Ranch in the 1940s, it was a civilized place with 500 people that had schools that taught in English, two grocery stores and even a pharmacy with a soda fountain and ice cream cones for a dime, not that I had any money, but things would soon change. At age 10, I would start my work career in a family owned grocery story for 50 cents an hour. I remember a lady giving me a 10 cent tip for carrying her groceries to her car. I will never forget what she told me: "Thank you. You are doing a great job." I was around 11 or 12 and this was the first time anyone had said anything positive about me. Over the years, I had developed a negative self image with poverty and limited education taking its toll. However, the mind is resilient and is capable at any time of entering into a new dimension. A word of encouragement, a positive idea, an inspiration from nature, a book, a movie, a dream or a teacher can change the direction of your life. My life wouldn't change overnight but the moment I heard the encouraging words, the process would begin.

Words Can Change Your Life

We have all read: "In the beginning was the Word" and from a religious perspective, the spoken Word has changed millions of lives. The lady telling me that I was doing a good job would gradually soak into my mind as well as something my adopted father told me which I will never forget. He would come home from work with dirt and oil stains all over his clothes and say: "Bobby, if you want to look like this all of your life, don't go to college." At the time, around age 10, I had no idea what he was saying. Sadly, I didn't know what a college was or where one was located, but over the years, the idea would begin to materialize in my mind and I knew that someday, somehow, someway, I would go to college. Looking back, these are the only two things I can remember that were positive words of encouragement except for a girl who said that she liked my hair. She was pretty but I never had a date until I graduated from high school. It's difficult when you don't have money or a car, and being ugly didn't help. The point is that the mind is beautiful and advanced beyond our age and maturity and is waiting, longing, for even a few words of encouragement. The mind is filled with unrealized potential (our greater purpose) and words of encouragement can trigger a breakthrough at any time to our conscious mind. Over time, my thinking would change. I am doing a good job. I am a good person. I will go to college. And my life would change. My love for my grandparents was rekindled as I would live with them in the summers and my dream of going to college would come true as I enrolled in Southwest Texas State College in San Marcos in September 1957. I would graduate and work as a teacher and coach in Blanco, Texas and later as a Methodist Minister in San Angelo, Texas. For the last 40 years, I have been a financial advisor in North Texas.

The Night That Changed My Life

Although I had been successful in professional life, I was unhappy with my life and temporarily lost interest in everything except finding a mate I could love and care for and work with me in business. I searched everywhere for six months, in yogurt stores, groceries stores and social hours with no success. I was praying, reading self-help books, communing with nature and even thought about going to church. Then, on March 31, 1989, it happened and my life has never been the same. I went to a private party at a restaurant and the moment I walked in, magic was in the air. I was standing in a crowd waiting to order when the lady next to me said hello and asked me to join her. Our eyes met for the first time and 25 years later we are still sharing our lives. We fell madly in love and married one year later on that same date and have seldom been apart since. It was a match made in heaven because I believe that God had prearranged our first meeting and was there smiling when our eyes first met. The moment I looked into her eyes, I knew that she was my Twin Soul, the love I had been searching for all of my life and 50 years is a lot of searching. She was my Twin Soul because she was a person just like me who had experienced all of the same things I had experienced in my lifetime without either of us knowing until we met and then it all made perfect sense. It was a dream come true and added an eternal dimension to our relationship. My heart instantly knew that we would spend the rest of our lives together and that God had brought time and chance together with a special purpose for our lives which we would soon discover.

Finding Your Greater Purpose

Working together for the past 25 years, Sheila and I have been successful in building a multimillion dollar company and are living a life that we could never have imagined or dreamed of when we were kids. The question came to our mind about six years ago: What are we known for in our local community? Making a lot of money? Driving fancy cars? Living in a million dollar neighborhood? Our childhood of poverty motivated us to do all this and more. However, both of us have always had kind, sensitive and passionate hearts to help other people and now we had the financial resources to give back to our community.

The first thing that we did was to have seminars for women at our country club providing financial education and guidance without the promotion of any type of sales. In our financial practice, we had seen many women with financial burdens from divorce, death of a spouse, credit cards, loss of jobs, and overspending with no money left for the education of their kids or retirement and our hearts went out to them. Over the past six years, we have created tons of goodwill with thousands of women who have attended our seminars. We are known as a couple that is passionate about helping the women of our community.

Our second program which is dear to our hearts is a scholarship foundation benefiting the children of our local firefighters and police officers. I personally know what it feels like to grow up in poverty with no hope of going to college or doing anything other than working and dying in the oil fields of South Texas. Thank God, that was not my destiny, but it has become my motivation to help kids who need a helping hand by providing scholarships for their education. Over the past four years, thanks to the donations from our friends, we have awarded 40 scholarships for almost $100,000. This year, our country club provided dinner for the students and their families with our mayor, city council members, state representative, district attorney, fire & assistant police chiefs with Sheila and I giving words of encouragement to the students. Some said that it was a spiritual experience with tears and hugs from the students and families when they received their $2,500 scholarships. Indeed, the tears and hugs confirmed in our hearts that this is our greater purpose in life.

Summing Up a Lifetime – Keeping the Dream Alive

God has appointed a time to be born and a time to die but until then, you must find and pursue the greater purpose that He has placed in your heart. This is your mission; your divine destiny and when it becomes part of your life, your life will never be the same. You will keep dreaming and making bigger and bolder plans and regardless of age, you will soar with the eagles and accomplish amazing things in your life. Remember, we all need to be loved, appreciated and recognized for the good things we are doing or simply for the good person God has made us to be. Part of your greater purpose should be in offering words of encouragement to everyone you meet. Your words can change the direction of a life, like it did mine when I was a kid. Simple words can change a life. You look great. I am proud of you. You are doing a great job. You are going to accomplish great things in life. I tell everyone I meet: Every day is a good day because it is the day the Lord has made and we should make the best of it. If we don't, who will? Your mission in life is to find and pursue your greater purpose of helping other people in some way, to always everyday offer words of encouragement and to secretly give to those who have special needs. Do this and God will bless your life and good things will always come your way.

My Wish For You

As you pass through this life, travel light. Pack your bags with only those things that are dear to your heart; things you can take with you into eternity. May your cares be few and your burdens light; and may the love of your life be with you when you take that final flight.

Heaven's Doors are always open to those whose lives are directed by a Divine Purpose. ■

Bob Johnson

Bob Johnson resides in McKinney, Texas and is a financial advisor with an insurance license and 63 & 66 Security Licenses. He focuses on tax strategies and retirement income planning. Bob began his education at Texas State University and became a teacher and coach. Later he attended ern Methodist University in Dallas earning a masin Divinity. He served as a Methodist minister before entering the financial services industry.

Bob enjoys teaching, coaching and inspiring his clients to "do the right thing". Bob encourages his clients to work hard, save, and to invest in the future. He stresses the importance of "giving back" along the way. Leadership by example is one of his personal characteristics and he guides based on his knowledge, experience and wisdom. Known for his slogan, that "every day is a good day", his clients are family to him. He also stresses the importance of goal setting and taking action to meet the goals.

Bob works with his wife, Sheila Johnson, who is also a Financial Advisor. They have two Cavalier King Charles Spaniels, Contessa and Duchess, which they adore. In 2009, they founded the McKinney Public Safety Children's Scholarship Foundation benefiting the children of their home town firefighters and police officers. Since that time, they have awarded 40 scholarships.

Bob and Sheila believe, "A Financial Plan can change your life and the lives of future generations".

You can make a difference!!

Bob Johnson, Registered Representative
JOHNSON INSURANCE & FINANCIAL
johnsoninsurnaceandfinancial.com
bob@johnsoninsuranceandfinancial.com
214.726.0000

3

Because Others Gave, I Give

By Tami Damian

It was Christmas Eve. Mom gathered her three youngest daughters around her. The girls were eight, eleven and thirteen. With great angst, Mom told them that this year Santa would not bring them gifts. The family was going through troubled times. Their home became too unsafe living with an abusive alcoholic. It was time that Mom took the girls away from their home, their small town, the state and their dad. They left with barely more than the clothes on their backs. The littlest one insisted on going back into the home they were leaving to get her baby doll. Even though time was of the essence in escaping town, she told her Mom, "I need someone to love me when I'm alone." They temporarily lived in an older sibling's basement and then moved to a small duplex in a town where things and people looked and sounded different than back home. In fact, the girls went from living in a place where everyone knew them, to a place that seemed like a foreign country.

They went from riches to rags in a car drive of fewer than 90 miles. The girls shared a bed in the basement. Mom slept on the couch upstairs. They had a donated Christmas tree, yet it looked bare with nothing underneath it. Mom planned stockings with small necessities for each girl on Christmas morning. Mom broke the news to the girls—no Christmas presents from Santa. The teenager stated that Santa wasn't real anyway. The middle girl was mad about everything in general. The youngest, the one Mom worried most about, looked up at her Mom saying, with her eight-year-old wisdom, "Mom, Santa doesn't care if we left Dad, he'll still find us." Tears brimmed in Mom's eyes; the littlest one kept thinking that they were the bad ones, for leaving. She wished the littlest one wasn't alone so much to take the phone calls from her drunken father. However, Mom had to work and get her GED; and the two older girl's school schedules kept them away. Mom placed the little girl on her lap.

"You're right. Santa knows that Daddy is sick and we had to leave for safety," Mom reiterated this message, hoping the girls realized that their father wasn't a bad person. Mom wanted the girls to understand that alcoholism was a disease. Their father, one of more than 12 children from a poverty stricken family, didn't choose this disease; it was part of his DNA. Mom continued, "This year Santa won't have enough for all the children." The middle girl angrily asked, "If money is scarce, why did you drop that dollar bill in the red kettle?" Mom knew this too was a learning lesson for the girls, one that would hurt, but perhaps carry into adulthood. "We had an extra dollar; certainly someone out there needed it more."

The middle daughter didn't concur, because right before the holiday break, there was no extra dollar to buy her teacher a present. The oldest just looked at the littlest girl, knowing this wouldn't help the nightmares. Unfortunately, the nightmares were based on the last days with their father. The teenager always cared for the little girl. She even had suitcases packed before Mom realized that they needed to escape. The teenager would do anything to protect her little sisters. Still on her mom's lap, the little girl announced an amazing faith and belief. "Mom, I know that Santa will come. I've been good. I know that he wouldn't forget us…I know he will be here…Mom, I believe."

There was little use arguing, because God knows, there was no sound reason why this happened. What kind of mother leaves a solid home, taking her daughters from a small town to this huge city? She had only pennies to her name with no education and little work experience. She quit school to have her first of six children with this man she loved dearly. As she told the girls, he was sick. The illness she could handle. It was the night that he almost took their lives that she knew she had to leave. The night he thought he was still at war and the family hid in an attic. She told the little girl to be quiet, and not talk. She was supposed to just hold her baby doll and make no sound. The little girl's silence probably saved their lives. Now, she barely talks. Mom taught her the lesson "Don't talk" too well. Mom asked the girl to recite the story of Rudolph, Santa's red nosed reindeer. It was on TV each year on the little girl's birthday. Through that story, the little girl understood the hurt of bullying; she told of Rudolph helping others even when he needed help himself. Speaking of the misfit toys, "If Santa brought those toys, I would love them like they deserve." The little girl recalled the scene when Santa announced, "I've got some bad news, folks. Christmas is going to be cancelled." Tearing up, she declared, "Santa never really cancels Christmas."

This little girl might have a hard life but she had such a soft heart. Mom could only hope that this soft heart would be used for good and not be used against her little girl. At bedtime she lovingly hugged and kissed her mother. Her words were, "Don't worry Mom, Santa will come…I believe." In the middle of the night, the little girl crawled upstairs to find her mother sobbing into a cold cup of coffee. She sat on Mom's lap comforting her. "Don't cry Mom. If Santa is too busy to show up tomorrow, he'll still find us. Let's believe together."

The next morning, the girls awakened, expectant and energetic and ran upstairs. The tree was bare underneath. Each had a stocking with an orange, an apple, assorted nuts, underwear and socks. Not the kind of presents that Santa brings. Ironically, they didn't even have a nutcracker. They later used a hammer. The two older girls were angry over the entire situation…leaving their home, their school and their friends. They were angry at having nothing and being made fun of by their peers. They were angry about receiving socks and underwear. But the youngest remained optimistic, "I believe.", she asserted. Late in the morning, someone knocked on the door. The little girl jumped up yelling "Santa, Santa!" Mom prayed that it wasn't her soon to be ex-husband, not wanting to call the police on Christmas.

Peering at present-laden adults, the little girl inquired who they were and who they were looking for. They worked for Santa they said...and they knew her name! YES! Santa is real! He didn't come, but he sent others. There were presents galore! Board games, robes for the girls, records, candy, perfume and more candy! It was the best Christmas ever! "See Mom," said the youngest, "If you believe it will happen! I told everyone to believe." Their mantra that day became—believe and what you need or want will come to you.

Mom began to believe too! Raising three girls alone proved difficult. Navigating public housing, food stamps and public health care were difficult trials. The youngest daughter always wanted and expected more. She hated the green lunch card that meant she received free/reduced cost lunches. Sometimes, Mom saved money so the little girl could buy chocolate milk like other kids. Mom knew how mean kids could be. She wanted to celebrate her elementary school's 50th birthday with a celebratory pin. Mom couldn't afford it, but one day a quarter appeared on Mom's desk at work with instructions to buy that pin so the little girl would feel proud. She was a Girl Scout, earning 'all around best scout' honors, selling the most cookies and raising funds for her troop. This was even though her family still had troubles paying monthly bills. Someone donated money for the uniform, sash and the badges she earned each month. Someone, somewhere, quietly gave so that this little girl could experience life. Each month a school book club order form arrived. She took home the flier circling every book she wanted to read. Most of the time, Mom redirected her to the library. Yet often, there was someone...someone that gave just enough for the little girl to order her books...sometimes she even got a free poster!

This little girl convinced the local newspaper that she could deliver newspapers at age 10, even though their minimum age was 14. She had her own checking account and learned about budgets early because someone trusted her. She conducted fundraisers at age 11 for those less fortunate. She proved responsible and reliable. And even though receiving help, she still helped others. She saved money to 'fit in' buying OP shirts, NIKE shoes and lunch from local vendors. Goodbye green lunch card. Although poor, she lived without shame; well not much anyway.

As the little girl grew, she played softball well enough to make a traveling team, but had no money to travel. Somehow, a parent always offered a ride, a room to share, and food from their coolers to feed the girl. Somehow, someone always helped Mom: by buying a ball glove, paying for a uniform, providing snacks and transportation. At 14, she defiantly said, "I will not live my life poor!" Mom wasn't angry, as welfare kept her kids alive. Mom was proud to see her youngest seek a different path. In high school, she needed a car for work and a car materialized. She wanted to join the spirit squad. There was no money. But someone gave. She had a uniform, right down to the right shoes.

Scholarships and grants were given so that the girl could attend college. She did. Mentors and older family members showed her how life can be lived when one does have money. She graduated. She decided to get a master's degree. She works today...and she gives. Today this girl's name is on a wall of benefactors to a community foundation, leaving a legacy. She established a memorial foundation in her Mother's memory. She works with other women giving money, time and talent to help children. She helps kids believe. She asks family members to ring the bell with the red kettle each Christmas season. She gives. She gives because others gave. Someone always believed in her when it mattered.

It's hard to imagine how life would have progressed for that little girl if 'Santa's Helpers' didn't show up that Christmas morning. Would she have lost her faith; turned cold and angry? What if no one gave money for her to partake in a school's party? Would she have become a loner and a hater? What if she wasn't allowed to compete in softball? Would she never have known the hurt of losing; the humility of winning; the pride of earning a trophy, the emptiness of coming in second, even though everyone played their best? What if she never had the joy of having her very own books? Would she have explored with the characters, realizing there was more in life than what she could see? What if no college scholarships existed? What if no one had believed in her, just as she believed in Santa all those years ago? What if she and her Mother didn't have that pact "If you believe, it can happen" What if?

We never really know the significance of our donated dollars, until perhaps many years later. The dollars and items donated throughout this young girl's life made a difference. They gave her something she needed to succeed. Hope. They gave her chances. They gave her opportunity. Sometimes the money that was donated took away the shame of being poor. Sometimes it gave her confidence, courage and faith.

It gave me life. I am proud to be the daughter of Rose Atkins. Fighter, survivor, care giver, supporter, Mom and believer. She gave me everything I needed and a lot of what I wanted. Sometimes I wonder how she found those donors, those agencies, those helpers. That I'll never know. But I do know...others gave...and they affected my life significantly. Because others gave, I give today. And I still believe in Santa Claus. ■

Tami Damian

Storyteller, teacher, trainer, author, advocate, friend, sister, aunt, wife, and daughter all describe Tami Damian, President of Leadership Education And Development (LEAD Group). Ms. Damian's passion is helping others find their passion and purpose. Tami has a way of seeing the strengths in others, and then challenging them to utilize and further develop their strengths. She also speaks for those that have not yet found or perhaps have lost their voice. She is a known difference maker in her community, volunteering for the United Way and several local non-profits. Ms. Damian is honored to work with major international manufacturing companies, developing their workforce, as the company implements quality, environmental, and occupational health and safety international standards. She is well respected for delighting her audiences with humor and presenting in a clear, easy-to-understand style, making potentially boring subject matter fun. Tami is one of twenty six first ever world-wide Certified Zig Ziglar Legacy Trainers. She is also the speaker and author of the Life Lessons Learned *series. "Life gives us the lessons," Tami says, "it's up to us to learn them."*

tdamian@LEADGroup.net
402-560-8264

HOPE: 10 Secrets of Finding My Way Back From Corporate America

By Alan Hunter

Most people believe that hope is wishful thinking, as in "I hope something will happen." That's not what I'm talking about. There is another hope; a better hope, something I've come to know as Confident Expectation. It's not just about believing in something; but knowing what is not yet seen is not only possible, but will happen. An example of this is a farmer. He doesn't just wish there will be rain and the plants will grow. He prepares his fields, anticipating that there will be rain, and expects to reap the rewards of his efforts. All of this is part of his thought process before he ever picks up the plow. Therefore, I wanted to let you know there is hope.

The Day That Everything Changed

Everything was quiet and suddenly I was awake. It was still cool and dark and as I gently wiped the sleep from my eyes and took a look at the clock. I couldn't believe I did it again. I woke up thirty minutes before my alarm. I was still awake tossing and turning at three o'clock in the morning. It took so long for me to finally go to sleep so how in the world did I wake up before it went off? Laying there ignoring the obvious, I watched those last few minutes tick by until the alarm finally went off. Of course, I immediately hit the snooze button like that's going to help.

After two; maybe three, snooze cycles I finally dragged myself out of bed and slowly made my way to the bathroom to start getting ready for my day. As I made my way through the bedroom I caught a brief but magnificent smell of fresh coffee brewing from the other part of the house and thanked God for my wife who made it and for the caffeine I'd be having as I drove myself to another day of drudge. Entering the bathroom, I flip and hear the click of the light switch and immediately feel the painful glare of the light as it hits my eyes. As I slowly gain focus, I lean forward and take a deep look into the eyes of the man staring at me in the mirror and then it happens. I can't stop what I'm about to say out loud "I HATE MY LIFE" which is immediately followed by "Where Did That Come From" as I shake my head at myself. I could write it off as a fluke or a temporary moment of insanity, but that was my morning ritual for several years.

As I headed out the door for the forty-five minute commute to the office I thought about how lucky I was to have my wife and daughter. They are truly the best part of my life and I am truly blessed. However, sometimes I feel like I've lost part of myself along the way. I used to have dreams and wanted to make a difference. But now all I want is to get through the day and to make it to the weekend, which always goes by so quickly.

I do have to admit that not all of the nineteen years that I worked for a major telecommunication corporation were bad. As a young man I had bought into the idea that a large corporation was the way to make a good living and provide a real opportunity to build a career. For a while that was happening. I enjoyed considerable success and was part of the fast paced telecommunications boom that took place in the 1990s and early 2000s. But then it happened; mergers and acquisitions, and changes upon changes. It seemed like things were changing every day and that you had to keep proving yourself over and over to another new group of executives who didn't know you from Adam and were only interested in their careers. In the end, I was stuck in a dead-end position with no hope for any future advancement.

As that day progressed it was much like any other day. There were calls to be made and deals to be done. But trying to get anything done amid all of the politics of the office was draining. As much as I hated it, I couldn't force myself to leave. I didn't want to start over somewhere else so I just kept plugging along. I figured that every business was the same. But sometimes God had other plans. It was about ten-thirty in the morning when my boss called and said words that I never expected to hear. She said that my position was being eliminated along with most of the other people in her group.

If you've been let go; downsized, laid-off, or part of an ever so great "reduction of force" then you know how shocking that can be. The strange thing was while I was a little shocked, I actually felt relieved. If you had asked me the day before what I would feel like if I got laid off, relief wouldn't have been my answer. My next thought was to go tell my wife. She actually took it harder than I did. I wouldn't say that I wasn't a little afraid too. After all, our income was about to be reduced by sixty percent. However, I felt something that I can only describe as excited calmness. I really believed that things would be alright and that it was God's plan for me to start a new chapter in my life. After all, his word does say "For I know the plans that I have for you declares the Lord, plans for good and not for disaster, to give you a future and a hope."

The New Normal

My last day in Corporate America was the day before Thanksgiving 2008. The one thing I did know was that going back to Corporate America wasn't for me. Instead I wanted to fulfill a lifelong dream to own my own business even though I had no idea what that would be. After taking a brief period of time off to get used to the "new normal" and doing some research, I decided to start a home improvement services business. I spent a year obtaining the needed licenses and industry certifications and bench marking best in class business practices from many home services companies.

Then on March 19, 2010, I launched Hunter Property Services, a swimming pool, irrigation maintenance and equipment repair company. My goal was to dedicate 100% of my time and energy to delivering first-class service to my clients. My philosophy would be simple: I wanted to put myself in their shoes and treat them like family. I would earn their trust everyday by treating their money like it was my money and by continually seeking educational opportunities that would allow me to provide innovative solutions for my clients.

I wish I could say the path I've been on the since that day has been easy, but it hasn't. My life is a continually improving process. I've never worked harder than I do now. However, the drudgery of all those days in corporate America was replaced by hope and optimism. This experience has taught me 10 secrets of finding my way back from corporate America. These secrets have changed my thought process and are helping me achieve my life goals. I believe they can help change your life too, especially if you want to start your own business. The secrets are:

Secret #1 - Take stock of your life experiences. There may be opportunities from experiences that you had earlier in life. During the summers while I was in high school and in my first year in college I worked for an electrician at my church. Joe Crane, the owner, who loves his wife and family, always encouraged me—sometimes with a swift kick in the butt—that I could achieve anything I put my mind to. He planted the seed that I could someday own my own business.

Secret #2 – Become a life-long learner. The most dangerous thing you can think is "I know that." Once you say that your brain shuts off. Always be willing to listen, even if it's a subject you think you know. You'll be surprised at what you may learn or realize that you may have forgotten. Adopting the attitude of becoming a life-long learner will dramatically change your life for the better. Most of my life, I didn't like to read, but over the past few years I've learned to love reading and learning. The goal is not to just study until you learn something; you should study until you can't get it wrong.

Secret #3 - No one can do it alone. You can't do everything yourself. The secret to success is building a team to support you. This includes the obvious like CPAs, lawyers, bookkeepers, bankers, employees, etc. However, it includes finding a great business coach(es). A good coach is someone who has done what you want to do. Not someone with theory, but someone with actual knowledge because they have done it. This is one of the hardest things to learn. The first step is getting the right coach.

Secret #4 – Learn Controlled Attention. Ever feel like you are spinning in circles with all of the things that you need to do? The secret is developing a habit of controlled attention which is spending time working on your business, not in your business. This requires scheduling time blocks throughout the week to focus on growing your business and not letting anything or anyone else occupy that time.

Secret #5 - Be around like minded people. I'm not saying you have to get rid of your old friends, your wife, children, the dog or anything like that. But you need to be around people who have the same types of goals and desires that you do. It will elevate your thinking and speed up the time it takes to reach your goals. This, along with life-long learning, will help change your mindset from one of being an employee to one of being a business owner. There is a difference; a big difference. Read "The E Myth Revisited" by Michael E. Gerber and let me know if you disagree—I'm betting you won't.

Secret #6 – Ignore stinkin' thinkin'. Zig Ziglar said "We all need a daily check up from the neck up to avoid stinkin' thinkin,' which ultimately leads to hardening of the attitudes." To take it a step further, you also have to avoid stinkin' thinkin' from others. That's right; don't listen to your brother-in-law, best friend from high school, or anyone else that hasn't done what you want to do. Their attitudes and opinions don't matter. It doesn't mean you don't still love them, but you can't let their uninformed thinking hold you back.

Secret #7 - Don't be afraid to fail. As John Maxwell would say "Fail Forward". Failures are learning opportunities; not definitions of who you are. Remember that a child falls down many times before they learn to walk.

Secret #8 – Dump the junk. You can learn anything you put your mind to, but sometimes it's better to hire someone with the expertise you need than to try to learn to do it yourself. Get rid of the time wasters. Focus your time on things that improve your bottom line.

Secret #9 – You should take possession of your own mind. Napoleon Hill said "you can achieve anything your mind believes it can achieve". The way to take possession of your mind is to control what you put into it. Remember, garbage in garbage out.

Secret #10 – Your business is your mission. This is the most important thing that I've learned. I was sitting in a conference and it came to me. My business is my mission. By following my mission, I will be successful and be able to achieve more than I could with just a job. I have learned that my business exists for one reason only; to achieve my life goals, which include helping others become all they can be. I can only achieve my goals by creating a turn-key business and I can only create a turn-key business by exercising controlled attention on the right things.

Final Thoughts

Life is way too short to wake up every morning saying "I hate my life" and heading off to a dead-end job. I'm thankful each day that God has provided me with the opportunity to pursue my mission in life and for bringing others into my life to help me discover the *10 Secrets of Finding My Way Back from Corporate America.* So don't be afraid to follow your dreams. Dare to be a difference maker because there is a hope; a better hope; a Confident Expectation of things not yet seen but that are possible and will happen if you take action. Remember it's up to you to live the life that God has given you – So live it. ■

Alan Hunter

Alan Hunter is the Owner/President of Hunter Property Services, a company that provides innovative swimming pool and sprinkler system solutions in the North Texas area. He understands his clients want to trust in the service professionals that provide services for their homes. Therefore, his philosophy is simple; put yourself in your clients' shoes and treat them like family. Alan holds a Bachelor of Science Business Management degree from the LeTourneau University, is a National Swimming Pool Foundation Certified Pool Operator (CPO), is an Association of Pool and Spa Professionals (APSP) certified technician, serves on the North Texas APSP Board of Directors, and on the Longhorn Irrigation Association Board of Directors. Today, Alan's focus is on building a turn-key business. He believes that when a business owner develops the right mindset and views their businesses as their mission, they have a unique opportunity to really impact their communities. He lives by the creed that his business exists for one reason only, which is to achieve his life goals and help his clients, employees, and community to achieve their life goals. To learn more about Alan and his vision for his business and other business owners, visit

Alan Hunter
HunterPropertyServices.com/manhoodplan Alan Hunter
alan@hunterpropertyservices.com

5

The Horrible Terrible Day

By Diana Corbin

December 29th was the day that our lives changed forever. That's where the clock stops. Life is never the same or means the same after that date. A car accident is what stopped the clock. Everything from that moment is measured by the timeline of the accident. Nate hit a tree, the only tree close to the road on the way home. Dylan had his seatbelt on. Nathan did not; neither he nor his older brother will wear a seatbelt to this day.

Grief is like a wound, a jagged stabbing knife through your heart covered in battery acid. It takes a long time to be able to breathe again. If you don't work thru grief—it will explode like a soda can that was shaken up and opened. We don't practice death. When we are faced with death we don't know what to do or how to deal with the horrible feelings and the future. Have you thought of the worst thing that could happen and pray that it never does? My worst experience was losing a child. I thought I could never survive it but by the grace of God I did.

This is my story. We were blessed with six kids—five by birth and a daughter came into our life for seven years through the foster care system. The best time of my life was raising our kids. I had always wanted a big family and was blessed to have one. Now we are enjoying our grandchildren and as people say there are nothing like grandchildren!! Our life was full, fast and busy. Our kids were involved in sports, 4-H, church and school activities. We live in the country in a small county were everyone knows your name. We only have two schools (an elementary school and a high school) so the kids are like family. Looking back, there were warnings. As my kids got their driver's licenses, everyone knew my mantra—buckle up and pray—it was weird. I don't know where it came from but I never failed to say it. Dylan was 16 and had just received his driver's license. I am so glad that he did because it was very important to him. They had tight curfews and were only allowed to go where they had permission. They always needed to call me when they arrived and when they left. Since the accident I have never thought to say it again.

The night of the accident was a very unusual evening. Decisions were made and actions took place that never happened before. It was just a few days after Christmas. I am a Dental Hygienist and worked late on Monday evenings. This was a Monday night. My last patient that day at work kept me until 7:00 pm that evening. He was a new patient and I am sure that he was the devil. He was the scariest and creepiest man I have ever seen. I have seen many patients but he made my skin crawl. I usually don't have those thoughts but with him I did. It was a pretty normal day. Don and I always knew our kids' schedule and talked about the next day at the dinner table the night before. It was basketball season for Dylan and sports and his girlfriend were what mattered. He had many friends and numerous opportunities for a broader social life but he would always choose to stay home and talk to her. My kids were very involved in school and activities and Dylan was no exception. He played football, baseball and basketball. He also had a girlfriend who he had cherished since grade school. He has always cared for her and she is an amazing woman today.

It was Christmas vacation and the kids were getting bored. There was a party that Monday night that Nate was invited to and Dylan asked if he could go (he never had asked that before). In fact, he was very insistent which was not like him at all. I was at work when they called to ask me about going. I was exhausted, it was right after Christmas and I did not have a lot of fight left. If I had been home, he would never have gone! The party was held by a senior (a classmate of Nate's) and Dylan was a sophomore. As I later found out, the party girl's parents were out of town. It turned into an ugly mess. There was a boy who cold cocked Nate in the back of the head because his girlfriend and Nate were friends. When this happened, Nate decided to leave and then realized that Dylan was in terrible shape. Nate had a couple of beers but Dylan had never had much to drink. He was tricked by some older girls who spiked his soda. As a result, he was wasted.

It was a funny trick, huh? There are many lessons to be learned. The party girls went to great lengths to buy a lot of alcohol. They crossed into West Virginia and bought the alcohol because the drinking age is 18. Once they were back in Virginia, one of the girls used her sister's ID to buy beer at a grocery store. The clerk did not like the ID and asked her manager who let them buy it. The girl's father, who was having the party, brought over a gallon of vodka. Her parents were divorced and her mother was away for a week. As you can imagine, there were many kids in trouble after this.

This loss, like all losses, was widespread. It cut deep and still does. The news was broken to us by Dylan's basketball coach who was also a state trooper supervisor. The first trooper was unable to deal with this terrible event since as I said everyone knows each other here. When Gary was responding to help, the new trooper he only knew it was two brothers. There were several sets of brothers that he coached. My husband and Kara had fallen asleep on the sofa waiting for the boys. When Gary knocked on the door she heard it with no filter. It is tough stuff for a 12 year old to hear terrible news about your best friend and closest brother. To this day, I still have terrible flashbacks when I hear someone suddenly yell my name. My husband ran upstairs and called me and I asked if everything was OK and he said no. Everything was never OK again. At 3:00 am, I began telling my children that they had lost a brother.

The armies of angels began to show up. Don's two best friends were at our house by 3:30 am to take us where we needed to go and to help us as needed. By the grace of God, there was a flight paramedic home visiting his parents who ran the call with the rescue squad. They were going to take Nate to the local hospital. However, he said that he needed to be flown to a shock trauma hospital. Fortunately, he was being taken to one of the best. This hospital was two hours away with no traffic and only 20 minutes by air. Nate spent eight weeks in the hospital and we were driven there every day.

Nate would talk about the bright colorful lights and the people yelling and dancing outside. He asked to please shut the curtains at the hospital and tell them to be quiet. We, of course, saw nothing. He would ask what they were doing. At first, I thought it was the lights of the landing pad for the helicopters. There was always flight traffic but when they moved him to another room it kept happening. It was months later when I realized he was having flashbacks to the night of the accident and seeing and hearing the rescue squad working hard to save his life. He was flashing back to the lights, loud conversations and the running around.

I later learned Dylan was having some interesting conversations with his friends. One of his best friend's moms told me about a conversation he had. She was nervous about telling me about the table talk in her kitchen that day but I am glad she did because it was comforting. She told me about two months after he passed that one evening when she came home from work to find Dylan and her son sitting at the kitchen table talking. It was nothing too unusual, she said. As she was preparing dinner, she heard a conversation that got her attention. Dylan was telling her son that when he died he wanted to have his funeral on the football field. Dylan was not one to talk about death. He was way too busy living his life and enjoying it!! Football and baseball were everything to Dylan—so the comment about the football field was very heartfelt. It was even more meaningful because the day after his death, I asked the principal if we could have celebration of Dylan's life on the football field. A total of over 1,000 people attended the event. I had no idea about the earlier conversation. (You can see why Dylan's friend's mom was a little nervous when she told me her story). Another conversation Dylan had with a friend was about smoking in the cafeteria at school one day. He was sitting with another best friend, who smoked and was telling him he really needed to quit smoking because he was an athlete and had a long life ahead of him. Dylan was not normally one to give advice on health and life lessons!

One day I was coming downstairs and rounded the corner into the kitchen. Dylan was sitting at the kitchen table with his football jersey (number 19), eating breakfast and studying for an exam. School was very important to him. When my eyes caught him there was a white light glow all around him like he was illuminated. It was beautiful but scary. He looked like an angel. He said, "Mom, what's wrong? I shook my head and said oh nothing—wanting to shake the sight away. There was an army of friends that helped us over several months. They provided food, friendship, love and support in so many ways. They moved into the hospital. The hospital said that they never seen such friendship with any other patient's family.

After the accident, I knew that I had a lot of work ahead. I had other children who would need me, an elderly mother and a husband who almost did not survive the loss. The longest journey would be helping a son that would have a long, hard recovery ahead, both emotionally and physically. My husband was Nate's Superman and worked hard at keeping him alive. Our dogs kept my husband alive. They would wrap him with their bodies around his chest and heart and neck, soak out the grief and fill him with love. God has a hand in all that we do because if he did not I would not have had any strength. In Matthew 6, it says "He will carry you when you cannot walk" and he did for quite a while.

Nate's injuries included a broken neck, a right ear that was almost severed, and bronchi tubes that were ripped from his lungs, a severe concussion, internal bleeding and bruising. The concussion had made him pass out while driving. His trauma doctor wondered why his head injury was opposite the side of the accident. The fight at the party explained that. I kept waiting to hear what Nate's blood alcohol level was. After a while, I finally asked. His main nurse looked at me funny and showed me the front of his huge chart. She said that information would be there but it wasn't. They usually find out right away on the helicopter but she said that there was nothing of any interest. The accident was caused by the concussion that he suffered at the party. The take away from this is not to let your underage children drink even at home. We did not, but the girls who held the party did. Don't stick up for your kids—there were many kids at this party whose parents went to the commonwealth attorney's office and asked that their child not get in trouble. This is a small town and favors were granted. The parents of the host of the party were never questioned. Kids did get charged with drinking underage and the boy who beat up Nate did get charged with assault. It was a cheap price for a life.

I am not at all discounting the drinking. Drinking and driving is a terrible problem. His hospital stay was extensive. After being released and allowed to go back to school, he wanted to finish his senior year. He continued to play soccer. He won a commercial baking and pastry contest and competed on the national level placing fourth in the entire United States.

Then he crashed and tried to burn. He spent several years trying to drink himself to death. The great news is that Nate has been sober for four years. He shares his story at least monthly with middle and high school students. Dylan was an organ donor, so please sign your card. Organ donation saves lives and changes lives. There are over 300 items they can use. For almost 10 years we have practiced holidays, birthdays, vacations, and just plain getting and being together. It gets better slowly. ■

Diana Corbin

We don't practice grief! Grief is an emotion we are not comfortable with or want to experience. Her journey through grief started with the loss of her son Dylan. She is sharing her journey through grief to help others cope. She is showing others that we understand what they are going through and helping them through the journey. She is a wife, mother of five grown children and a grandmother of soon to be five beautiful grand kids! She has practiced Dental Hygiene for over 30 years and is now in Dental Education and Sales. Diana wants to dedicate this chapter to her children. She is a speaker and writer and can be contacted at:

nextlevelhygiene@yahoo.com.

6

Hindsight is 20/20

By Davina Ilgin

As mothers, we dream about, and idealize, our birthing experiences. I'd pictured my twins swaddled in soft flannel and gently placed on my breast to hold and to hug, ever so gingerly, because they'd be tiny and fragile. We'd bond instantly. I'd nurse them with ease while being enveloped in a mist of euphoria special to nursing moms. I'd nuzzle them lovingly while inhaling the soothing and tender fragrance that only babies emanate.

Not quite. My water broke early. The harsh reality of pre-term labor and an emergency C-section THREE MONTHS EARLY robbed me high and dry of this most precious dream.

Instead, my fragile twin boys, weighing less than two pounds, were quickly rushed upon delivery to the Neonatal Intensive Care Unit (NICU). I wasn't able to see them, nor hear their cries, because they couldn't breathe on their own. Alas, bonding didn't occur until several weeks later.

Both boys were immediately placed into incubators and wheeled off to the NICU. My husband accompanied them as I sacked down—sweaty, nauseated and totally exhausted—for my belly to be sutured back by my obstetrician's nimble fingers.

I never imagined this happening in my wildest dreams. My delivery was both beautiful in bringing our boys into the world, while also spiraling uncontrollably into a dreadful experience.

I felt cheated. Why had it come to this? Why did I go through months carrying our boys, dogged through a difficult labor with horrible contractions—only to have them ripped away from me and holding on to dear life! How could life deal me this unfair hand?

I questioned God and the laws of karma. Was God finally punishing me for all the bad stuff I've done in my life—the fake I.D., the under-age drinking, the lying and the stealing?

Even though the doctors told me it wasn't my fault, I still continued to blame myself. That's what mothers do. We rewind to every past event and keep replaying them.

"Oh, I shouldn't have danced at that wedding. I should've taken it easier and quit working. I shouldn't have had sex while pregnant." The list just went on, wearing me down emotionally—wearily and endlessly.

Tears welled up when I saw my boys with tubes and wires hooked up all over them. You'd think that I'd be desensitized from having worked in the NICU as a pharmacist, but I was unprepared and shell-shocked to see my own children in this situation!

I felt that they were suffering needlessly—and that it was my fault. Tension was building as I thought about every possible medical challenge our children would face during this time—and into the future.

I moaned and mourned—would they be handicapped? Although I hated to dwell on it, I pondered the possibility of losing our precious preemies. Why had it come to this? I wanted to see their first steps, hear their first words, celebrate their birthdays, teach them how to read, watch them ride their bikes and raise them to be kind men.

Coming home every day without my boys being there to greet me was awkward and painful. It just wasn't natural. I didn't feel like a real mother for weeks. I'd look at the empty nursery that my husband Rick and I had spent so many happy hours preparing—only to suffer teary meltdowns.

I'd dream about the day that they'd come home, always hoping it'd be sooner than what I was told. But it only hurt me more.

I remember the doctor calling me one early morning, "Mrs. Ilgin, I'm so sorry, but Milan had a turn for the worse. We had to put him back on a breathing tube. I am so sorry." I hung up and started to cry hysterically. All those thoughts about bringing them home, all those dreams of celebrating their birthdays went out the window. My knees fell weak and buckled. I was brought to my knees in sorrow. I instinctively started to pray.

I was so engrossed in what the future would bring that I failed to see each day and each hour as the gift it really was. From then on, I found it was better to focus on each day as it came, instead of living for the unknowable future.

Hindsight is always 20/20. I now realize that the journey with my boys struggling to stay alive in the NICU is when my own spiritual journey started. I learned my biggest life lessons from our NICU trials and triumphs.

I learned that challenges are there to bring us back to consciousness or to the spirit of God—whatever you want to call it. When we are disconnected from the Source, sometimes what we perceive to be a negative life experience may present itself. In this case, it was my boys being born prematurely. This crisis put me back in the present moment and in alignment with the Spirit.

Hearing my boys' cries and watching them literally fight for their lives on a daily basis brought me to my knees in prayer—for the first time. I learned to finally relinquish control and have faith in God.

All the guilt that I felt was actually holding me back. We think that if we feel guilty, we are attempting to be a better person. This is far from true. Guilt is like the alarm going off in the building—it's not going to put out the fire, it's just going to be the alarm.

Before I delivered my boys, I remember being "worried" about paying our mortgage on time and making sure that the nursery was painted and all ready to go. I fretted about how my boss would react if I decided to stay home with my kids. I worried about losing the baby weight. I worried about how we were going to care for our twin boys with no family in town…and the list went on and on.

Well, once my boys arrived three months early, all of those previous "worries" seemed senseless and a waste of time. The only care on my mind now was their health. God was teaching me about gratitude. Each day in the NICU I learned to be grateful for our basic victories—my son being able to breathe on his own; clear of any infections with no brain bleeds, etc.

I learned that life will always challenge us. We shouldn't turn the challenges into problems. A challenge is something we are capable of overcoming and once we do, we feel accomplished and have grown as a person. A problem is something that stands in our way. There is no self-growth and there is no sense of accomplishment. I once saw our NICU experience as a problem, but I now see that it was just a challenge.

Every challenge happens for a reason. It is there to teach us an important lesson. It's up to us to figure out what the lesson is.

Our boys were finally released home after fourteen grueling weeks in the intensive care unit. We continued to face many obstacles—surgeries, sicknesses, therapy, and the list goes on. Raising preemies has been the most difficult and most humbling experience in my lifetime. I have grown immensely as a person and mother.

All of the trials that we've faced have only made us stronger. I emerged a stronger person emotionally, physically, and spiritually. I realized my importance as a mother and, in the process, discovered my "big why": to use my experience and knowledge to uplift, support, and enlighten other mommies.

After having gone through every imaginable emotional up and down of roller-coasting the NICU, I am confident that I will be able to handle every challenge that life brings my way. I wouldn't change any of it. And I am grateful for all of it. Amen to that! ■

Davina Ilgin

DAVINA ILGIN is an author, Certified Life-Coach, and earned a Doctor of Pharmacy degree from Purdue University. But she is first and fore-most, a mother. She lives and breathes her motto, "Let's change the World…one mommy at a time."

Her three amazing boys were the impetus to founding the Mommy Life Coach Academy, where mothers learn to be the best mommies they can be and have a positive impact on their children, and ultimately the world.

Davina believes wholeheartedly that our job as a mother will be THE MOST IMPORTANT job that we perform in our lifetime. After all, we are raising the future. We are shaping the lives of our children who are the future leaders and decision-makers of the world.

Through specialized programs, home-study courses, and one-on-one coaching, Davina and Mommy Life Coach Academy help mommies around the globe do our very best. When we grow as mothers, we raise better kids. By raising better kids, we change the world. IT'S THAT SIMPLE.

Learn more about Davina and Mommy Life Coach Academy and get your FREE Parent Guide, "How To Really Be A Super-Mom" at www.MommyLifeCoach.com

Be sure to follow Davina on Twitter and Facebook for parent inspiration!

Davina Ilgin
mommylifecoach.com
mommylifecoach@gmail.com
twitter.com/MommyLifeCoach
facebook.com/MommyLifeCoach

7

Practice LLP and Boost Your Profits!

By Jim Palmer

One of the most important and powerful business building lessons is what I call LLP, which is not a legal term. LLP stands for Listen, Learn, and Profit. To do this effectively, you have to retrain your ear, because, first of all, people are very busy. We have electronics all over the place including cell phones, iPads, and multiple computers. All of these things are vying for our time and attention.

The rapid growth of my business in large part has resulted from me practicing LLP and listening closely to the 'pain' points and desires of my clients. Here's a quick story that illustrates LLP. When I started my first business in October, 2001, it was called Dynamic Communication and I was writing and designing newsletters for companies, associations, non-profits, and chambers of commerce.

I would write and design my client's newsletter and then get paid for it. I started learning that this wasn't the best business model. When their newsletter was done, unless they chose to do another issue, which was not always guaranteed, I'd have to go and find another client. However, I did this for five years and developed a pretty good business, or at least a nice income.

However, I learned something very valuable while I was in my clients' offices. I kept hearing how it took them too much time to write and put together their own monthly newsletters. They also never knew what type of articles to include in their newsletters.

Coming up with the content was a problem for them—a pain point. It was around this time that I started learning about Internet marketing and wanted to find a way to leverage my skills and talents for creating profitable newsletters. However, instead of getting paid by one client at a time—I have multiple clients that pay me!

In 2006, I started my second business which was my first online business—No Hassle Newsletters. With No Hassle Newsletters, I put together all of the content that a fun, informative customer newsletter should have and started offering it to businesses around the country. Right off the bat I started getting monthly subscribers!

As my online client list grew, I started getting feedback like, "Jim, we love the content, and *our customers love to read* the content you provide us." As a quick educational side note, this is officially LLP lesson number one. When this particular customer said, "Jim, my customers love reading your content," I went and trademarked my articles as "My Famous Customer Loving Content." What a great tagline and trademark—all because I listened!

The next part of the LLP story is when a few of my clients starting saying, "We have a hard time getting designers to design newsletters the way you say they should be designed. I thought, *Okay, there's another pain point and an opportunity to create another revenue stream!*

I created my now famous "Done-for-You" No Hassle Newsletter templates. My No Hassle Newsletters are already filled in with content and are ready to use. Using these templates, my clients can put out a monthly newsletter in less than an hour each month. This is another example of where I heard the pain point and added more value to the program, allowing me to raise my monthly fees.

In November, 2008, while exhibiting at a national marketing conference in St. Louis, one of our clients came up to our booth and said, "Jim, I love the newsletters, the content, and the ready to go newsletter templates that you provide, but we have a hard time finding and working with printers who understand the way that you suggest the newsletters should be folded and mailed. They also don't know how to work with the mailing list. Do you have any suggestions or can you make a referral?"

What I heard was another customer pain point and that spells opportunity! My choice was to make a referral or, better yet, create a solution that adds another revenue stream and that's what I did. Less than sixty days later I launched The Newsletter Guru's Concierge Print & Mail on Demand Service. We now print more than 40,000 newsletters a month for my clients. So when they do their No Hassle Newsletter, they just send us their newsletter mailing list, pay for the quantity they want, and then we do the printing and mailing. They never even have to leave their desk or talk to anybody on the phone.

In November of 2012, I had more than one request from my now hundreds of clients to refer them to someone who can do some article writing. Since I employ several writers, my choice was to make a referral—or (you see it coming!)—create another solution and revenue stream. In January, 2013, I created and launched my Custom Article Generator Service! My clients can now get a custom article written for them on any topic for a great price! Are you starting to see the power of LLP?

As you can see, every single one of the additional businesses and revenue streams that I've created were a result of me listening to what my customers were telling me and asking for. I listened to their pains and desires, learned how to solve their pain by adding more value and in the process, I've added multiple revenue streams to my business.

You can also absolutely do this. When you can hear and address the pain points and desires of your clients or your prospects, and you solve their problems with what I call world-class service, you're not only going to create additional revenue streams in your business, you're going to create more raving fans and customers for life.

So listen, learn, and significantly boost your profits! ■

Jim Palmer

Jim Palmer is a marketing and business building expert and the host of Newsletter Guru TV, *the hit weekly Web TV show watched by thousands of entrepreneurs and small business owners. Jim is also the host of* Stick Like Glue Radio, *a weekly podcast based on Jim's unique smart marketing and business building strategies. Jim is best known internationally as 'The Newsletter Guru'—the go-to resource for maximizing the profitability of customer relationships.*

Jim is the founder of Custom Newsletters, Incorporated, which is parent company of:

No Hassle Newsletters
No Hassle Social Media
Success Advantage Publishing
Concierge Print and Mail on Demand
Custom Article Generator
Double My Retention, and
Infographic Generator.com

Jim is also the acclaimed author of five books:

The Magic of Newsletter Marketing – The Secret to More Profits and Customers for Life
Stick Like Glue – How to Create an Everlasting Bond With Your Customers So They Spend More, Stay Longer, and Refer More
The Fastest Way to Higher Profits – 19 Immediate Profit-Enhancing Strategies You Can Use Today
It's Okay To Be Scared – But Never Give Up
Stop Waiting for it to Get Easier – Create Your Dream Business Today

Jim Palmer
TheNewsletterGuru.com
800-214-6158
guru@thenewsletterguru.com

8

The Silver Lining

by Danielle Noel Hawthorne

I remember "the moment" very vividly—making the conscious decision right then and there—to ACT instead of react. I took a page out of Kathleen O'Connell Chesto's book, "Risking Hope: Fragile Faith and the Healing Process," written after she was diagnosed with Multiple Sclerosis. I found great strength and comfort in a three-word phrase that I had read, "WHY NOT me?!" With that thought foremost in my mind, I threw my arms wide open and chose to embrace the journey that was about to begin.

When I was just 31, I was diagnosed with breast cancer. Admittedly, I was stunned—being the healthiest, most fit person that just about anyone knew—with no family history.

I enjoyed the many blessings of having grown up on a small organic farm in upstate New York. I worked hard and played hard. I was an active competitive athlete since childhood and COMMITTED to a healthy lifestyle. I was a non-drinker, passionate about personal development, a lifelong learner, and DRIVEN by the desire to make a positive difference in the lives of others daily.

My conscious DECISION was to seek out the silver lining in this major life challenge and to ask the Universe to help me remain teachable through everything that was going to come my way. With the added benefit of having lived the prior 10 years "one day at a time," I was armed with a tool kit brimming with positive attitudes, productive action, acceptance, courage, wisdom and faith. I knew that I had gathered the necessary resources—and network—that would help me to navigate the maze of doctors, procedures, emotional upheaval and physical pain. In my heart of hearts, I BELIEVED that it was going to be an incredible journey—a life changing one—and my guiding prayer was to have the privilege to pay it forward. I distinctly remember thinking, "When I get through this I'm going to help other people face their life challenges…" by sharing the amazing learning lessons that I knew I was going to collect along the way. I didn't know the "how" but I did know the "why".

There was another important decision that made a huge POSITIVE impact on my outlook—my team of doctors. We took a partnership approach to determine my course of treatment. I chose the most aggressive one, the one that would cause considerable side effects but also had the highest probability of SUCCESS! The doctors were charged with eradicating the small, temporarily ill, part of me as fast as possible while I turned my daily focus to maintaining my financial, intellectual, physical, emotional and spiritual wellbeing.

How did I do that? One of the ways was to take positive ACTION. For instance, I knew that I would be losing my long, brown, wavy mane of hair. It was my favorite feature and super hard for me to come to terms with. So, I went on the offensive. I counted the days after my first chemo treatment, knowing that between days 10 and 12 it would start to fall out. And it was about the 10th day that it began to happen while I was in the shower. I realized that I better stop washing it or it would all be gone! I threw on my USA baseball cap, my ponytail sticking out the back, and headed out to a party at a friend's house. Later that same evening *it was time.*

There would be no "victim" in this scenario. I wasn't going to allow the cancer to "take" my hair from me. I decided to be in

CONTROL of the transition to my new "Ms. Clean" look. I chose to shave it off! My friend, Mindy, agreed to do the honors. It was an incredibly surreal but also very EMPOWERING experience. During the last few passes the buzzing of the electric razor became seemingly louder as the chatter slowed until there was silence. The reality of why we were doing this began to sink in and when the mission was complete I asked for privacy. It took a few moments before I stood up and turned to face myself in the mirror. Much to my delight I discovered my head was a good shape and there weren't any weird bumps. That, and my big smile, was all I could see.

The next morning I stepped out into the world sporting my new "do" with pride. My best friend, Sandra, even bought me cool tattoos to emblazon the sides of my head before soccer matches. That really impressed the little kids. I'd be in a store after we played—I played no matter how lousy I felt from the chemo, I just kept putting one foot in front of the other—and I'd hear whispering, "Oooooo, that must have really hurt." Then there was LAUGHTER...my own! I found every opportunity to laugh and right out loud. It's very true what they say—laughter is the best medicine—and I knew it would help me HEAL.

I remember how I felt when I joined my Brooklyn gal pals on a sunny September Saturday in New York City to celebrate the birthday of our mutual friend, Joanne. We gathered at her favorite restaurant, AMERICA. During dinner one of the servers came over and slipped me a note on one of their paper napkins that read, "We think you look amazing." Now, they didn't know why I had chosen the Sinead O'Connor look, they probably thought it was INTENTIONAL. What they didn't know is they were right but for a reason unknown to them. I still have that napkin.

Fast forward to almost 10 cancer-free years. I'd been diligently working toward achieving my life's dreams and goals while FULFILLING my promise to serve God and others daily.

I'd been blessed to share the decade-long journey with my partner, Robyn, in our little grey house complete with white fence, a beautiful Australian Shepherd, Jamoca Almond Joy, and our two cats, Jasmine and Max. All was right with the world! Until, it wasn't. This would be an even greater life-threatening challenge.

I found myself suddenly dealing with an unexpected and very serious cancer recurrence that my surgeon and oncologist identified through my routine blood work. And although it was evident that I was sick again, there was an added CHALLENGE of determining the type of cancer and finding exactly where "it" was hiding. Test after test after test, then a PET scan, followed by a needle biopsy through my ribs and into my chest—which was the singular most painful procedure that I have ever been through to this day. I remember counting to two hundred and then I started to PRAY, calling on those who had already crossed over, my maternal grandparents, Aunt Joan, and best friend, John, to help me. It took everything I had to stay on that platform so the doctors could finish. WE did it.

It was two days after my birthday and I was sitting in my oncologist's office looking out the window when I was given the news that the cancer was inoperable. You know that saying about your LIFE flashing before your eyes? I experienced that. The tears streamed down my face as I sat there in shock and watched the leaves slowly flutter down from the trees.

Once again it was time to rally my SUPPORT system—family, close friends, doctors, a few select colleagues—even an occasional stranger. I drew strength from the many gifts I had received the first go round—acceptance, courage, wisdom and knowledge, a resounding internal fortitude and an even greater FAITH in God. Combined with consciously *living life on life's terms* for 20 years I was ready, we were ready, to be victorious once again!

That Christmas I invited all of my immediate family to CELEBRATE together at our home. My Mom and Dad traveled from Rochester and stayed with us at our house. My sister and her family drove down on Christmas Day while my brother and his family joined us via Facetime. As we all sat downstairs gathered around the tree, we shared stories, opened gifts and laughed. I was keenly aware of every moment, it felt very surreal, almost an out-of-body experience. My faith ebbed as I watched the festivities and my thoughts drifted to, "Is this going to be my last Christmas ever?" I worked to refocus and find my ATTITUDE OF GRATITUDE. That helped me to remain present and to cherish the forever memories we were creating as a family. But the fear still lingered at the edges of my mind that it could be the last Christmas with my whole family.

It did turn out to be the last Christmas...for my Dad. We unexpectedly lost him the following August, six days before his seventy-third birthday. Had I not been faced with a second cancer battle we would not have all come together for what was his final celebration. I am so GRATEFUL for the holiday spent together that even if I were given the chance I would never change the second cancer diagnosis. I had found my silver lining once again.

We are all faced with daily challenges—ranging from insignificant to life threatening. Take a moment now to identify your level of satisfaction with how *you* respond to them and if you're happy with the outcomes. Do you act in a positive and CONSTRUCTIVE way when difficulties arise? Or do you react from a negatively charged or emotional state? Making the choice to be PROACTIVE in your thought process, decision-making and plan of action puts you in the driver's seat and provides peace of mind.

Through my life experiences it had become crystal clear to me that thoughts and language (conscious, subconscious and unconscious) had a direct and immediate impact on my internal and external environments. They could be powerfully PRODUCTIVE and constructive—a potent combination that promotes PURPOSEFUL action. Or, they could be a destructive and counter-productive force—becoming a proverbial wrecking ball and catalyst for negative behaviors. The key was to choose carefully what to THINK, what to DO, what to SAY and how to say it—all I had to do was "PAACE" myself!

I formalized The PAACE™ Principle: Positive Attitudes and

Actions Create Evolution, and combined it with my holistic approach to healthy living I call, FIPES™: Financial, Intellectual, Physical, Emotional & Spiritual Wellness Strategy. Implemented in tandem, it's a powerfully effective method to attain EXCELLENCE in every focus area of life. And together they became the foundation for my BlogTalk Radio show, "30 Minutes of Mojovation." A live online syndicated program that I developed to attract listeners who wanted to learn how to take charge of their journey and develop strategies to achieve the life they desired and deserved.

On my premiere show, one of the questions an audience member asked was, "How do you stay so optimistic and positive all of the time, especially during your two cancer battles?" The answer was simple: PERSPECTIVE and GRATITUDE. Along with maintaining positive attitudes and actions! It's easiest to illustrate using a simple, real life example.

Returning from a business trip to Charlotte, I was informed that there would be a three-hour delay. It meant that I might not make the 7:00pm event that I was scheduled to host in Connecticut. While waiting for my flight, another passenger who realized the delay meant she was going to miss her Boston connection struck up a conversation. Her stress was not only visible in her face and body but also palpable in her language. She was one big ball of verbal and physical negativity! Neither of which was going to change the OUTCOME of the situation.

How did I deal with the delay and my impending absence at the event? I put The PAACE Principle into effect and:

- CHOSE to stay relaxed, emotionally and physically.
- LEVERAGED the time and took action to catch up on my work.
- POSITIVELY projected out to the Universe my desired outcome.
- BELIEVED all would be well.

After landing at JFK I jumped in my car and drove home, made a quick stop to change, and arrived just far enough in advance to hurriedly prep for the event. I was ready for our guests right on time! The funny thing that was unbeknownst to me was that everyone who confirmed they'd be in attendance had cancelled for one reason or another. So, after all that…no one even showed up! It was just one of my team members and me sitting there.

So, what did we do?

- IDENTIFIED that we're powerless over people, places and things
- CHOSE to see the challenges we had been given as opportunities for growth.
- MADE a gratitude list of all the things that came out of not holding the event
- LEVERAGED the time and brainstormed for upcoming events

It doesn't matter if it's a broken shoelace, a broken heart or you're just plain broke. The more FOCUS that's given to the perceived problem, the bigger it becomes. But if the choice is made instead to focus on the SOLUTION, the more obvious it becomes. And by applying The PAACE Principle you have the power to pursue and manifest positive outcomes.

I'm blessed to be here to write that it's 18 years after that first life-changing day and I'm now a three-time cancer surTHRIVOR! And although I'm still recovering from the recent surgery I know more will be REVEALED on this journey. I just need to "give time, time."

I'd like to share one final thought, something my good friend Stacey Connor said while driving together to a motivational seminar a few years ago, "If there weren't any speed bumps on the roadway of life, I'd fall asleep at the wheel!" Remembering that moment still makes me laugh right out loud. How I cherish my many precious FRIENDS.

Thank you for sharing in my journey. May you always find your silver lining! ■

Danielle Hawthorne

Danielle "MOJOVATOR" Hawthorne is a three-time cancer surTHRIVOR, entrepreneur and visionary marketing professional. Her success connecting brands with their core markets and target audiences through innovative, integrated, multi-channel strategies spans two decades. She recently certified as a Small and Medium Enterprise (SME) Coach for the largest global loyalty rewards program, Lyoness. Danielle developed The PAACE™ Principle: Positive Attitudes and Actions Create Evolution, *and teaches clients how to create the life they desire and deserve. A seasoned speaker and host of "30 Minutes of Mojovation", she shares her real-life journey, insights and proven success methods to help others pursue and achieve lives of abundance.*

Danielle Hawthorne
mojovate@gmail.com
facebook.com/MOJOVATOR
twitter@MOJOVATOR
linkedIn.com/in/danielleMOJOVATORhawthorne
203.520.1000

9

Life in the Foggy Lane

By Julie Bartlett

Have you ever experienced a moment when life felt *foggy*? It is as if you have been ripped off course and can't get off 'auto pilot'. Life is passing by at a supersonic rate and…there you are… stuck trying to figure out what you are 'supposed' to be doing, how you got where you are, and how to get focused.

Feeling like this one day too many finally got my attention. *What was I focusing on?* I was so fuzzy that 'it' was hard to see clearly. I thought that if I could just bang my head up against a wall then all of those thoughts would get in line. I would know which ones were the real trouble makers and weed them out. The problem was that life wouldn't stop so I could take action on my plan. Instead of banging my head against the wall, I decided to turn to one of my favorite Bible stories to help me stop over-thinking and possibly give me some peace of mind.

I knew I was taking an unwanted trip down *foggy* lane and wanted to change the course towards clarity. Have you noticed that there comes a point when 'why am I here' isn't a simple question anymore? To serve others isn't a good enough answer because it's incomplete. It empties me without the guarantee of fulfillment and value. I wanted it all. I wanted to know that what I was doing was fulfilling my purpose, that I was valued, and that the natural outcome would be of service to others. I needed to take that complex question of 'why am I here' to God.

One of my favorite ways to gain insight is to read my Bible. This time, I needed Joseph. Though I can't remember the exact age that I first heard of Joseph, I do remember that I immediately liked him. His story intrigued me. What first struck me was that he seemed larger than life simply because he seemed to possess a strong inner compass that was always focused on his purpose. His struggles could have taken him off course so I returned to Joseph's story to have a moment of peace in order to gain insight and strength.

Being the youngest of eleven boys, and only 17, Joseph wasn't taken very seriously. Nonetheless, his brothers hated him as Joseph was their father's favorite and being a bit of a tattle-tale didn't help him earn their respect. Joseph was given a varicolored tunic—a coat of many colors—by his father. The symbol of favoritism only sealed his brothers' jealousy.

This didn't deter Joseph from sharing his dreams with his family. His first dream included him and his ten older brothers binding barley sheaves in the field. His barley sheaf stood tall while his brothers bowed to Joseph's. His second dream had the sun, moon and eleven stars all bowing down to him. His brothers and father scoffed him for these dreams, but that did not stop Joseph from deeply believing that his dreams held a special meaning.

It didn't take long for his brothers to take advantage of an opportunity to harm Joseph when he found them in a town, far from where they were supposed to be. They saw him and began to plot his death. Their plan was to kill him, throw him into a pit, and then claim that a wild beast devoured him. Why? It was to put an end to Joseph's dreams.

The oldest brother, Reuben, discouraged the death plot. Instead he suggested that they throw Joseph into the pit and leave him. Though Reuben planned to later rescue Joseph, in his absence, the brothers decided to sell Joseph into slavery. *Genesis 37* (Ryrie Study Bible, NAS)

Each time I read this story, I discover something new. But, for years I wondered how Joseph's story and mine had anything in common. I didn't have dreams of greatness and I've never been sold into slavery. Joseph's life was so different from mine. Does his life seem different from yours? Are you sure?

No, I've never been sold into physical slavery, but I have been enslaved to certain negative mind sets and heavily impacted by the negative mindsets of others. Just like Joseph. Surely, he experienced some *fog*, too! So what did Joseph do? How did he respond? And, can I repeat his actions?

Joseph's owners brought him into Egypt and sold him to Potiphar, an Egyptian Officer to Pharaoh. Joseph did quite well at Potiphar's house, quickly finding favor and becoming head over everything that Potiphar owned. Everything seemed to going well for Joseph until Potiphar's wife decided to pursue him. The woman was in serious pursuit and Joseph's character really begins to become clear. He refused her repeated advances. She falsely accused him to her husband, and Joseph landed in jail. Not the local jail, Pharaoh's jail. *Genesis 37:36 – 39:20* (Ryrie Study Bible, NAS)

Oh, good. It was more drama. Joseph's story was getting real. His life took a sharp turn which jerked him into a new reality—one that he wasn't pursuing—and this path seemed to take him farther away from his dreams. When would it get back 'on course'? What's the point of this struggle?

You know Joseph is super frustrated. I can imagine Joseph wanting to snap at everyone 'in his way'. He had to be wondering if his dream was nothing more than just a fantasy. Seriously, God, when is something good going to happen? When would the tide turn toward Joseph, instead of against him? I know this feeling.

As much as I'd like to fast forward to the end, I know that the real story is in the middle of the chaos. Not so much the chaos itself, but who Joseph is becoming during the chaos. Whether he created the drama or not, he has a life lesson to learn.

What happens when you focus on the chaos instead of the lesson? Do you linger in the chaos? Create more chaos? Perhaps the chaos isn't really chaos but part of the lesson. Maybe life isn't the adventure you want or thought it would be, but it can still be an adventure. The fog can lift.

The kindness of the Chief Jailer putting Joseph in charge of all the prisoners and then not micro-managing him because Joseph's efforts were blessed (*Genesis 39:21-23* NAS).

Joseph served two years in prison. Maybe it was another delay. Can a prison be a training ground for leadership? Could this physical prison represent his emotional prison? Could Joseph be a very happy guy, right now? Betrayed by his brothers had to be hard to get past. Betrayed by his employer had to be hard to get past. What lesson did Joseph need to learn? Humility? Anger management? Forgiveness? What lesson do you need to learn so that you can be the person who can fulfill your purpose?

Purpose isn't just about doing something great or achieving a certain place. Purpose is intentional and firmly rooted in being or becoming the kind of person who can hold that place with authority. Who was Joseph becoming during his imprisonment? Who are you becoming?

One day, three of Pharaoh's servants joined Joseph in prison. At this point, Joseph was practically running the prison since the jail keeper trusted him so much. Obviously, Joseph's management skills were being sharpened. But there was something else going on, something else that would help him not just be a good manager but a great leader.

Joseph's new jail mates were Pharaoh's former baker and butler. Joseph took care of these two guys and one night, they both had dreams. The next morning Joseph found them looking rather dejected so he asked why. They told Joseph that their sadness came from having no one to interpret their dreams. Joseph responded that "all dreams belong to God" and suggested they tell him their dreams.

For the butler, the dream interpretation gave him hope of being restored to Pharaoh's court. But for the baker, the dream revealed his demise. Three days later, this is exactly how it played out. Unfortunately for Joseph, the butler forgot about him for two years. Then Pharaoh had a couple of dreams of his own. (*Genesis 40-41:1*)

I really have to hand it to Joseph. I'd be an emotional mix of hurt, insulted, and mad about being forgotten. But Joseph didn't seem angry about all the delays. Maybe Joseph was learning patience.

Maybe he was learning humility—and forgiveness. Joseph's character was being transformed and sharpened so that his life legacy would reflect mastery of these character traits. What does seem to be getting clear is that Joseph was getting clear about who he needed to be no matter his circumstances.

How good are you at patience, humility and forgiveness through the delays and betrayals? Are you patient with yourself? What's on your entitlement list? Who do you need to forgive?

I've had moments of humility. There is a difference between real and false humility. Real humility comes from love and recognizes that everyone has value and everything has its time and place. We are not all on the same journey or in the same place along the journey. Life has greater peace when you focus on who you are called to be and forgive yourself when you don't. Which signs are you focused on each day? Is it confirmation that you're learning the lesson or that you're stuck in the *fog*?

The story of Joseph is a beautiful story of a boy whose internal compass became clearer through his struggles. He started life with a firm grip on the knowledge of having his father's favor and trust in his childhood visions. But his life became meaningful as he chose patience, humility and forgiveness as the keys to lifting him above the fog in order for his dreams to come true.

Joseph knew he had his father's favor. Do you believe you have your Father's favor? You may or may not have a physical father to associate with this kind of love or feelings of value, but don't stop there. Forgive. Let God take that place. Letting God be God allows you to be clear about your focus—where you are and where you want it to be as well as whom you are and who you want to be—no matter the circumstances.

Periodically, I go on a 'Joseph Pilgrimage'. Every day, throughout the day, I consciously remind myself that I have My Father's favor. In fact, it's one of my affirmations. I always feel a shift inside of my heart and my mind. Within seconds, I feel so loved and valued! In fact, this single exercise has a wonderful impact on my ability to allow others to know that they, too, are loved and valued. It's easier to respond out of love and not obligation. Life has more hope with love. Love gives me permission to let go of the fog and replace it with clarity.

Joseph was learning his lessons and holding on to his dreams while he was imprisoned. Little did he know just how abruptly that his circumstances would change.

Pharoah's dreams needed an interpreter and Joseph was ready for the job. At the age of 30, just 13 years after his brothers sold him into slavery Pharaoh made Joseph the second most powerful man in Egypt. It would seem that in the blink of an eye, Joseph's life took a dramatic turn toward his dreams being realized. But it was those lessons learned that helped him be prepared.

Seven years brought great harvests to Egypt, then the drought hit. Eventually, the drought was felt by Joseph's family and his brothers travelled to Egypt. The brothers didn't know that they were meeting with Joseph as many years had passed. And Joseph didn't know if his brothers had changed since he last saw them, so Joseph tested his brothers.

Joseph accused them of being spies and threw them into prison for three days. On the third day, he told them to return home and bring the youngest brother back as only then would he release the remaining brother. The brothers, talking amongst themselves and not knowing that Joseph could understand them, believed that they were being punished for what they had done to Joseph so many years ago. (*Genesis 41-42:23* NAS)

I think that his brothers were burdened with guilt. Guilt is a heavy burden and a debilitating master. Joseph couldn't trust that guilt was a motivator for his brothers to make better choices. He had to know he could trust them and forgiveness allowed him to test them out of love. Joseph was not obligated to forgive them nor was he obligated to help them, but he wanted to and he wanted to do these things out of love. He wanted to be very clear that love and forgiveness would show up in their new relationship.

As commanded by Joseph, nine of Joseph's brothers returned to their father to bring the youngest brother, whom Joseph had never met, back to Egypt. This was not an easy conversation for the brothers to have with dad. The father, still mourning over the loss of Joseph, wasn't eager to release his youngest son. But to have his elder son return home, he had to.

The brothers passed the test. Joseph finally revealed himself to them. They wept. They embraced. When Pharaoh learned of Joseph's brother's arrival, he insisted on the entire family moving to be near Joseph. (*Genesis 42:24- 45:28* NAS).

Joseph's dreams came true! But while the dreams showed his family bowing down to him, they didn't tell the whole story. Joseph's story isn't just about his beginning dreams or that in the end his dreams came true. Joseph's story was bigger than that.

Joseph was a different guy by the time that 13 years of slavery ended. I'm thankful that Joseph had his walk through the *fog*, like me. He never compromised his character and held tightly to the fact that he had his father's favor and he had his dreams. In spite of all the struggles, disappointments, and seeming impossibilities, Joseph grew into being a man of great influence. Along his *foggy* lane journey he learned to choose patience, humility, and forgiveness and he found love. His dreams came true.

How about you? Would going on a 'Joseph Pilgrimage' help you to reduce the *fog* and focus? Will you let God be God while you choose out of love to give yourself permission to get good at patience, humility, and forgiveness? Are you ready to shift off the foggy lane and onto a clear path?

For the next 30 days tell yourself 'I have my father's favor'. Every night write down three things you are grateful for about yourself. Ask God who you need to forgive, including yourself. Forgive out of love and set yourself free. Thank God for specific signs of kindness that you experienced that day. You are priceless, worth choosing well for, and have a purpose that no one else can fulfill. As the *fog* lifts, you'll see it and you'll be fabulous always! ■

Julie Bartlett

Julie Bartlett inspires purpose-driven success in others. As a Professional Brand and Image Coach and Speaker, Julie combines her extraordinary range of talents to evaluate, educate and motivate those going through a life or career transition.

Whether advising clients who are seeking their own personal style, pursuing a new job, going from divorce to dating, or losing weight, Ms. Bartlett ***first*** *leads her clients to find and embrace the power, beauty, and style already possessed within. She then creates a customized wardrobe that reflects the clients' distinct expression of who they* ***really*** *are and how they want to be seen in the world.*

She is founder and CEO of Colour IQ, a Dallas, Texas-based consulting firm that empowers clients with the tools to ***"Be Fabulous Always."***

Julie Bartlett
colouriqstyle.com
Julie@ColourIQStyle.com
214-223-2200
facebook.com/pages/Colour-IQ/111359262526
linkedin.com/in/juliebartlettcolouriq/

10

My Hope Lives On

By Yvonne Howdyshell

I stepped uneasily through the back door of the little church. A funeral was about to start and I did not belong there. My unkempt appearance and bloody nose were evidence of that. The organ music played a melody meant to soothe as the tears of family and friends flowed, but I didn't have any tears left. My tears had been replaced by determination. I could not stay in my house for one more day. I slipped onto the organ bench beside the woman I hoped with all the world to one day be able to call "Mom." She and her husband were my earthly saviors, the two people who took me in when my world was unbearable.

Mike was the preacher at the Staunton Church of Christ and Pam, his wife, served alongside him. The funeral service was difficult for Pam as she waited until its conclusion to ask me what happened. Because of our history and her understanding of the living situation with my biological parents, she had suspicions. After the grieving family and friends had moved down the aisle and out of the building, she ushered me out in the parking lot and into her car. There I told her the whole story. There had been an argument at home. I'd been hit in the face by a broom and chased down the street. "Oh, Honey, you are safe now; I can promise you I will see to it that you never have to go back!" she said as she put her arms around me.

That day was one of the turning points in my life. My story started eleven years earlier. I was born into the home of two of people who were the worst imaginable match for one another. Ross was 48 when they met. He had lived a hard life, becoming an alcoholic early, working temporary jobs in construction and barely getting by. Ruth was 25 and suffered from mental illness diagnosed as paranoia schizophrenia. She was hospitalized for the first time at age 17. Shock treatments and other primal methods used on the mentally ill never solved her problems and most certainly created more. Medications helped, when she took them consistently.

They met while both living at The Beverley Hotel, which had once been a grand establishment in the little town of Staunton, Virginia. Through the years it had fallen into disrepair and had become a sanctuary for those who were down on their luck and couldn't find their place of permanence in society. The town was home to a state mental institution, Western State Hospital, as well as a prison. After discharge or release, many who had lost homes and families due to their circumstances stayed in the town and found camaraderie in the company of others who shared their plight. Ross and Ruth found each other there.

Before long, she became pregnant and they were married. I was born on September 4, 1968. Within four months of my birth, Ruth was admitted into Western State Hospital. Ross was unable to care for me and asked Mr. and Mrs. Madden, the present minister and his wife at church to take me in. The Maddens kept me for awhile but feared that they were becoming too attached to me. They asked Social Services to intervene and I was placed in a temporary foster home until a long-term placement could be found. That placement came with the very loving family of Mr. and Mrs. Rexrode. They loved God, each other, their daughter, and then me.

I only have pictures and home movies to tell the story of my life there, but I have seen enough to know it was a warm, loving, secure place where "normal" family memories were made. We took trips to the beach, played in the snow, read bedtime stories, and shared a beautiful life. I came to know them as my family and they gave me all the things a child needed in those critical early years to feel safe, secure and loved. Eventually, Ruth was released from the hospital and visitations were arranged. I have pictures of that, too. The scene includes the only woman I had known as a mother, Mrs. Rexrode; my biological mother, Ruth; and a social worker who held me while I looked discontented and not at all certain or secure. I lived with the Rexrode family until I was almost three. They wanted and tried to adopt me.

In keeping with the notion that a child is best with his or her biological family, custody was granted back to Ross and Ruth with stipulations that visits to the home would happen frequently to assure that I was cared for properly. We lived in the basement apartment of a house on New Street. Maybe that name was symbolic of a new beginning and a promise of hope. For awhile, things looked up. My understanding of this time has been pieced together by reading the reports of a visiting social worker. Her words create a picture of a sweet family, one where I was a thriving little girl with shiny blond hair who shared cute stories about what I did with my parents. Ruth spent considerable time reading to me and this appeared to be one of my favorite activities. Developmentally, I was progressing well and the social worker was very pleased with my progress.

We moved to a house on Frederick Street when I was four and soon I started to attend kindergarten at Second Presbyterian Church in downtown Staunton. Ross worked in construction and Ruth cleaned houses. In kindergarten I won the coloring award more days than not with my best friend, Lisa. I remember walking home one day with Ruth and telling her that Lisa and I were bored with winning and we threw it off that day, just scribbling. I received a stern lecture about always doing my best, no matter the task. We attended our church every Sunday. The church had a bus ministry that traveled through my neighborhood, picking up kids whose families couldn't bring them. My parents always went on Sunday morning, but I wanted to be there every time the doors opened. I loved Children's Church. The people were so loving. I created a deep bond with each of my Sunday School teachers. Sometimes the bus didn't run, but that wasn't always communicated to me beforehand. Sunday and Wednesday evenings found me on the front porch steps waiting. When the bus didn't come, I felt such disappointment. Church was home to me and the people there were my extended family. I know that God put in me the deep desire for that place to be such an integral part of my life and I am so thankful for that time.

Without that, when the darker days came, I may not have survived. When I was in first grade, life changed drastically. Ruth decided that medicine was no longer needed. As Ross walked me to school one day, I asked, "Daddy, why is Mama so different?" In my six year old mind, she was mean, yelling a lot and she never seemed happy. He did not have a reply that soothed, clearly not knowing how to explain it to me. At home, they fought much of the time and became violent, often threatening to kill one another. There was a gun in the house which I found and hid so no one would be hurt. Ross' way of coping with the arguments was to binge drink. One morning I was awakened by a screaming match that escalated into a wrestling match. The altercation led to her breaking his leg as I watched.

As time progressed, my dilemma was that in Ruth's eyes, I could never do things right or well enough to please her. I bore the brunt of the cleaning and cooking responsibilities for the family and received a scolding when my efforts were not good enough. I dealt with physical abuse, mental abuse and attempted sexual abuse. Classically, I made up stories about marks and bruises. Looking back, the stories were outlandish. A mark above my lip caused by a hurled piece of ice was translated into a tree branch that fell on me as I looked up. People knew the stories weren't true, but no one intervened because everyone was afraid of my mother. She held anger in her eyes that appeared to run deep into her soul.

She had to return to the hospital and I was again taken in by a church family, the Campbell's. They made me one of their own and I relished living in a place where life matched the picture of what I dreamed a family would be. Upon Ruth's release, though, I was returned home. The honeymoon period did not last long at all, but God sent others to me and He used them to change my life forever. When I was eight, a young couple, Mike and Pam, came to our church. He was a fresh seminary graduate filled with expectations for his first full-time senior minister role. She was great support to him in every way, playing the piano, leading the choir, and sharing in the ministry in many ways. She started giving me piano lessons and they even found an old upright piano on which I could practice. They brought me to their house once a week, where I would sit at the kitchen table and do my homework while she fixed dinner. It was so peaceful there. My shiny blond hair had turned into a stringy mess. She washed my hair and set it on rollers, making me feel adored and pretty. We had races while doing the dishes to see who could finish first, the one who washed or the one who dried. He teased me and gave me hugs and showed me how a godly man acted. We had dinner around the table each time I went, talking and laughing. No one yelled at me and I could meet all of their expectations.

This place, these people, and others, God used in my life to teach me to hold on for something more. God's hand on my life never faltered. For a while I had to endure pain, but just as the words of the poem *Footprints in the Sand,* I am reminded that even then, I was never alone. ...The Lord replied, "The times when you have seen only one set of footprints, it was then that I carried you." – Mary Stevenson

Amid the sanctuary of spending time with Mike and Pam, my other world unraveled completely. Ruth again went off of her medication and it seemed the older I got, the worse it was. I wanted out so badly and one day, when I was eleven years old, my wish came true. While sitting in the living room, watching afternoon cartoons, Ruth came in and told me to get out. I had asked earlier to go to a friend's house after school and was told I could not go. She later said that when she told me to leave, she meant for me to go there. I am not sure, but my understanding at the time was to leave, period. It was Halloween. I walked several blocks to a little family grocery store on Beverley Street and called Mike and Pam. He picked me up and took me "home".

Before long, Ruth was again admitted to the hospital. I stayed with them for two and a half months and it was heaven for me. Behind the scenes many adults in my life were talking about who could take me in. It had become apparent that I could not live with Ross and Ruth. That year, I spent Christmas with Ruth's sister, Yvonne and her husband Charles. They lived in Manhattan with abundant wealth and material belongings and would have loved me and raised me as their own. My heart, though, was with the people at the church parsonage who, with a minister's salary, had barely enough to get by. Down to my core, I was homesick for them. After Christmas that year, I went back to them.

On January 11, Mike's birthday, I was summoned to the principal's office for a visit with the social worker. Her shocking news carried words I never wanted hear. I thought I was safe forever and I would never have to go back to Ross and Ruth's. I was wrong. That very day, my belongings were packed and by dinnertime, I was back. Fear and utter sadness gripped my heart. For the next few weeks, nothing was right with her. The new clothes I had received as presents for Christmas were shoved in a closet with chastising that "Now, you think you are too good for us." She could not be pleased and held an ever-present rage. Her mind took her to an altered universe where she thought she was Jesus and she convinced herself that she was blind. Her paranoia was evident as she told me that ghosts would come out of the walls to get me and many other scary tales. No matter what I did, I could not make it better. Ross and Ruth argued all the time and many times he left to drink as an escape. I could not escape and lived in anxiety and dread. Mike and Pam called daily and I whispered on the phone about how terrible it was, hoping that Ruth would not catch me talking with them and fearing retribution if she did.

Eventually, when it became too much, I found my way to the church and slipped onto the organ bench beside Pam on that fateful day. I have blocked out much of the difficult experiences and barely even remember walking there. Pam and Mike took me in and I was able to find a forever home. Our bond grew to what seems like that of biological parent and child as they helped me grow up and past the hurts that I had experienced.

Life hasn't been perfect since then. When I was seventeen, Ross died alone, having divorced Ruth after I was taken away. He wasn't found for several days and I struggled with guilt over that. He had finally found sobriety through a renewed dependence on God and the help of Alcoholics Anonymous. Through the years, he called and I saw him occasionally. I know that he truly loved me, but the choices he had made before I was born carved a deep rut in his life that took a long time to overcome.

Ruth continued to have trials. She escaped one night from Western State Hospital and was hit by a car. The physical toll that took on her body and brain left her changed forever. She married a man who was very abusive to her and eventually divorced him. I know this because we found each other again when I was in my twenties. From then, until she died a few years later, we forged a relationship, fragile at best and full of heart ache for me, but eventual healing was found, too. One thing I realized through that process was that she wasn't able to remember the bad times. I think they were not present at all. I know that she had a ravaging illness and lived in torment herself. She loved me and did not intend to be so hurtful.

That realization did not come easy to me, but I thank God that through time and the love of others, He has allowed me to understand. I am grateful for the last memory I have of her, a viewing at the funeral home. There for the first time, her countenance was peaceful as she did not have to struggle anymore. Death brought a respite that she never found in life. My life, is to me, a miracle and

I hope to make a difference by sharing how God's hand was in my life from the beginning. Mike and Pam finished well the job of raising me. They adopted other children, each coming with their own nature and baggage, which created trials in our family, too. However, Mike and Pam were and are the love of God to me. He used them to save me emotionally and physically.

That coupled with His eternal salvation make me who I am. I have married an incredibly wonderful man, Bradley, and we work daily through the challenges and joys of marriage and life together. He is such a blessing in my life. My beginning did shape many things about me but does not define who I am today. I have become an educator and through that field seek to "pay it forward" to all of those who poured into my life—teachers at church and school, foster parents and other encouraging adults. There were so many that God used. I don't have to tell students or staff my story. But when I know they feel that life is overwhelming or has given them more than they think they can bear, I hope to be a support and comfort. I, too, have lived in the darkness. I thank God for bringing me to a place of marvelous light and hope. Last year, my husband and I started mentoring a nine-year old child, Jaylen. He has had many challenges and lives with his elderly great-grandmother, the only family member who could or would take him in. This relationship has been such a blessing to us and his grandmother asked us if we would become his godparents. We agreed and when I told him that he would one day live with us, I shared a bit of my story and of the forever home I found at the age of eleven. He was happy to know that we would be his parents and replied, "Wouldn't it be neat if I came to live with you when I am eleven and then when I grow up, I could do that for another child who needed it?" It certainly would be "neat" and I could not ask for anything more! ■

Yvonne Howdyshell

My roots are in the Shenandoah Valley, specifically Staunton, Virginia. I attended James Madison University, hold an undergraduate degree from Mid-Atlantic Christian University and a master's degree from Shenandoah University. In addition to working in Christian Education, my career includes teaching and administration in public school systems at the elementary and middle school levels. My passion is to make a difference through relationships and encouraging young people to hope for a greater future. Bradley, my husband, and I currently live in Scottsville, Virginia, where we own Thacker Brothers Funeral Homes. Bradley operates the funeral homes and I work as an administrator at Fluvanna County Public Schools. We often joke that we don't have two-legged children, rather the four-legged variety. One of our "kids", an Italian Greyhound named Giuseppe, is too spoiled for his (or our) own good but is a great companion and friend. His little sister, Sadie, a miniature Doberman Pinscher mix, was a feisty addition to our home through a rescue foundation. She keeps Giuseppe running and us laughing. We look forward to the day when we can provide that forever home to our godson, Jaylen, and pray that God will bless our family. Until then, we hope to serve Him faithfully and to make a difference wherever He calls us.

Yvonne Howdyshell
y.l.howdyshell@gmail.com
1496 Dobby Creek R.
Scottsville, VA 24590
(434) 953-7891

11

From Hitler to Hollywood

By Elizabeth McCullough

I'll bet that title got your attention. Well, this chapter is not about a dictator travelling to "Tinsel Town". It is all about your dream and the pioneer spirit within you. Sit back, relax, grab a cup of tea and let's settle in together for a few minutes of storytelling. Oh sure, I would love to get you all fired up and ready for action, but first let me share something that will inspire you to dig deep and act on your purpose, your dream and your heart's desire. We will "connect the dots" at the end of these tales.

This is a story about the "pioneer spirit" of American people. It follows four different families from far away countries who settled here for a better life. Each one shows extraordinary courage, faith and passion as they take on huge obstacles in order to make their dream come true. From Germany came the little girl whose courage to stand her ground forced them to escape Nazi rule using a New York City bus pass. From Ireland came a family who refused to fight against their own and took political asylum in the new country. From Holland came an inventor who solved a major production issue for an American icon. From England came the most graceful, tender and beautiful young woman. Ruby accomplished her dream of becoming a ballerina, joined the Russian Ballet and decided to stay in New York while on a world tour. How the four families come together is an amazing tale of unlikely pairing and circumstance. Why they came together is a story of passion, courage and daring to follow your dreams. It doesn't end there... they go on to live the "pioneer spirit" in extraordinary fashion. That special "something" shines on through future generations. However, those stories are saved for another day.

J. M. Ganvoort brought his wife and children from Holland to the United States of America in order to provide a good life for them. He was a good and reliable provider. The family even brought the old traditional Dutch painted shutters and built a house from the ballast of the ship in upstate New York. Life was grand for a while, but at some point the marriage dissolved and Mr. Gantvoort established himself in New York City as a well-known inventor. A brilliant and talented man, he was focused on problem solving. When the National Biscuit Company had a production issue, Mr. Gantvoort had an invention under patent to solve that problem. Until then, commercial bakeries used a conveyer belt to run pastries through a convection oven. When the equipment broke down, production came to a halt until it was fixed. Mr. Gantvoort's invention would allow several ovens to connect so that if one went down they could pull that one and fix it without interrupting production. The National Biscuit Company enjoyed tremendous success and is now known as Nabisco. Yes, J. M. Ganvoort invented the cracker oven for Nabisco. He is my grandfather.

Hilde Heinze took a huge leap of faith to make her dream come true. She left her family behind in Germany and crossed the Atlantic Ocean to find freedom and independence in the United States. She was making a new life for herself at the tender age of 22. Hilde found employment in New York City working for Mr. Gantvoort. They worked closely, fell in love, got married and had a daughter named June. The poor child was born with severe asthma and spent much time in the hospital. There is no greater suffering for a loving mother than to see her child struggling to stay alive and grasping for each breath. After careful consideration, Hilde decided to take her daughter back to Germany where her sister's husband was a well-respected doctor. She knew that he would provide the very best care for June. However, letting go of his little family was devastating for Mr. Gantvoort who was left behind to run his business. He could only hope they would come back soon, but that was not to be. An evil dictator came into power in Germany which changed everything. It was too much for Mr Gantvoort to bear. After considerable heartbreak and suffering, this brilliant, passionate, genius of a man decided to take his own life. With one gun shot on Valentine's Day...my grandfather was gone.

Hilde and June lived with the Futter family in a beautiful home. Young June had a play-house and a pet deer in the back yard. They enjoyed the comforts and spoils of a good life...for a while. Suddenly, they found themselves trapped in Nazi Germany. This family did not ask to be a part of the most evil reign of terror. It just happened. Not to take away from the Jewish people's suffering, but even Christian citizens were forced to comply or to pay the consequences. The soldiers took what they wanted, when they wanted and demanded loyalty to Hitler. Unfortunately, Dr. Hans Futter lost his house to the Nazis simply because they wanted it. He had the most beautiful home in the area and was the only one with modern, electric appliances such as a refrigerator. The whole family was displaced, forcing them to find food and shelter where they could. On occasion, the Nazi soldiers would parade through town expecting every citizen to "Heil Hitler"! Having seen what these soldiers had done to her family and home, a rebellious little girl named June refused to take part. She would not raise her arm! She would not say those words! When pressed by the soldiers, this small yet courageous child became loud and intentionally spoke in their tongue. "Ich bin ein Amerikaner!" she exclaimed. Hilde quickly tried to excuse her child's behavior by explaining that June was sick and didn't know what she was saying. She pleaded for and was granted mercy that day. Knowing that all children were expected to declare loyalty to Hitler by age 10, Hilde understood that they had to find a way to escape from Germany very quickly. By the grace of God, she was able to fool soldiers at the gate with her New York City bus pass. Although forced to give up her U.S. citizenship in order to live in Germany, she had hung onto this bus pass which had her name and photo on it. She risked her life, but it worked! Hilde is my grandmother and June is my mother.

The Gribbon Family

They rushed to the shore in the middle of the night. This was the last they would see of their beautiful home-land as it was shrouded in darkness. Counting heads and staying close together, the Gribbon family clutched their few belongings and scurried onto the boat that would deliver them from "the fight". Crossing the Atlantic was a long and uncomfortable journey, but they were free from the oppressive rule forcing brother to kill brother in Ireland.

Taking political asylum in the U. S., they were free to follow their dreams.

Skip a generation and you'll find the Gribbon brothers clowning around for a living. The funnier they were, the better it was. Entertaining in the new world had become a respectable form of art and they were darn good at it! Charles, Harry and Eddie Gribbon worked alongside all-time great comedians such as Charlie Chaplin, Fatty Arbuckle and Buster Keaton! They did vaudeville in New York City, became the Keystone Kops and moved to California where they made dozens of movies. Sister Florence was also in the business, but "Auntie Floss" was more involved in the production end and at one time owned a film storage warehouse in Fort Lee, New Jersey. Still, she was just as much a Gribbon as the rest of them. They laughed, played, drank and were a very jolly family. Their parties were legendary and no one would have guessed from where they came. Charles Gribbon is my grandfather.

Ruby Clark

Ruby Clark was born in London, England. Although she was a proper, kind, gentle and respectful young lady with Christian values and her morals intact, all she wanted to do was dance! This tiny ballerina and her best friend "Vi" joined the Russian Ballet Troupe and toured in the U.S. Ruby decided to stay in the new country and married one of the Gribbon boys. She and Charles enjoyed show business and followed the entertainment industry from New York City to Hollywood. They were in silent movies and even a few "talkies". Their careers were short-lived, however, as they decided to start a family. Ruby and Charles settled in New York State to raise their two boys named Charles and James. Ruby is my grandmother.

As a side note, please search for the 1940 Charlie Chaplin movie, "The Great Dictator". Note that my great-uncle Eddie Gribbon played the "Tomanian Storm Trooper" in this movie. Now isn't that just a weird twist of fate? One branch of my family tree has unwittingly made a movie about the other branch's life. It was crazy. But that is what being American is about. We come from every corner of the Earth and have been given an amazing opportunity. We are free to make (or break) ourselves. You are your only obstacle. It's your life, own it!

So far you have read about real people who have overcome huge obstacles in order to make their dreams come true. They took action, took a risk and made it happen. They crossed oceans, lost loved ones, looked evil in the eye and made this world a better place. You can, too! What is your obstacle? Is there an ocean between you and your dream? Are you oppressed or depressed? What is stopping you from doing that thing that is on your heart and mind? Do you think you can do it later? How much later? Do you have some magical guarantee that you will even be here later? No? Then get started! Now!

If you are living in the great United States of America you already have it better than 97% of the world's population. Look at what you do have, not what you don't. I know you have at least two good eyes if you are reading this chapter.

Look around and find your resources. They are all around you. You don't need a lot of money, just a little time. Be creative. Carve out and schedule a little piece of each and every day to work on your dream and go do it! Wake up a little earlier or go to bed a little later. Designate that as your "action time". This little piece of time is dedicated to making your dream come true. The first step is the hardest, but I am challenging you to take that leap.

Good luck. Now, go get 'em! ■

Elizabeth McCullough

Elizabeth McCullough is an award winning entrepreneur, former owner and operator of an international fitness and weight loss franchise location, long time chamber of commerce ambassador, and author of several projects including the upcoming book "From Hitler to Hollywood".

She has a wide range of experience from working in the financial industry to food service and from child care to horse training. Always one to follow her dream, Elizabeth has enjoyed checking off her goals one by one. The lifelong dream of writing her own book is about to come to fruition in the very near future.

Ms. McCullough's work has been published in Texas A&I University's "Writer's Block", she penned a monthly article in "South Texas Living Magazine", was featured internationally in the "Diane" magazine and has written many press releases over the past decade.

She was General Manager of four very successful Curves franchises for six years before purchasing the one in her home town in 2007. At one time, she was managing 23 employees and 2, 200 members in a tri-county area. Ms. McCullough enjoyed the status of Multi-Franchisee of the Year in 2002 and Manager of the Year in 2003.

In addition, she has supported many charitable organizations such as Toys for Tots, American Cancer Society's Relay for Life, Coastal Bend Blood Center, MDA, Driscoll Children's Hospital and Coastal Bend Blood Center. Liz McCullough has been a very successful fundraiser, cheerful donor and will roll up her sleeves to help when needed.

Elizabeth McCullough
elizabth_mccull@hotmail.com

12

Stab the Monkey!

By Tami Fenton

I have a mission in life. It's pretty simple and very good, even though it sounds horrible! But if you'll adopt this mission, I promise it will change your life, and the lives of those around you for the better. My mission is to stab the monkey! Before you call the local zoo and post my picture let me explain. You've heard the old saying, "He's got a monkey on his back!" When I was a kid that meant some poor soul had a drug or alcohol addiction. I've come to realize that the monkeys on most of our backs are much more insidious, and easier to hide. Some of my personal monkeys were extreme shyness, clinical depression, and lack of self-esteem.

So, how do you stab a monkey? I'm glad you asked. It's as easy as taking any immediate action to stop the self-defeating voice in your head. Some people will imagine a big red X. Some may actually hold up a hand to express, "Stop". I've even read about having a meeting with your negative voices and telling them to knock it off. I, however; imagine that voice as a monkey riding on my back, whispering lies in my ear. Then I imagine yanking the screeching thing off my back and stabbing him to death, with the sword of truth. I keep it holstered in the scabbard of justice on my right hip. Because he's a metaphorical monkey, he just vanishes in a magical poof of lavender smoke. I would never, ever harm an actual living, breathing monkey. Once the monkey is gone, I stand taller. I literally feel the weight lifted off of me, I sigh in relief, and I move forward!

We pick up these monkeys in the most innocent ways. When I was seven years old, my family went to visit my aunt. As often happens between older people and kids she asked me, "Tami, what do you want to be when you grow up?" I guess she believed that every self-respecting seven year old should have a complete life plan. I piped up and said, "I want to be a model." I had recently attended a charm and poise school which culminated in a fashion show where each of us walked the runway modeling merchandise from a local children clothing store. My seven year old self believed that I had modeled fabulously. I incidentally was chosen to model a coat instead of a pretty sundress, but that's a story for another time. My aunt began to laugh heartily and said, "Oh, honey. To be a model you have to be real pretty." Welcome to my back, "you're not very pretty monkey". Seriously? From the time I was seven I believed that I wasn't very pretty, and that really sucked. The coat choice suddenly seemed logical.

The winter of my 11th year my family went snow skiing. I'm not particularly athletic. Honestly, that's an understatement. I'm particularly non-athletic. That's more appropriate. If you ever have the misfortune to see me try to throw or catch a ball, you'll have pity for me, and understand exactly what I mean. I was, of course a disastrous skier. My waterproof ski pants were so wet from falling in the snow that I was made to sit on a towel in the car on the way back to the lodge. When we arrived, it was decided that we should all pose for a picture with our skis. All except for me, because only the good skiers should be in the picture. Ouch! And thus another monkey.

Before I trek too far down memory lane, let me ask you this important question. Who has labeled you, and therefore saddled you with a monkey? Sometimes our parents, teachers, siblings, and friends give us lifelong monkeys. Sometimes we create our own. But however we acquire them, the monkeys are still there. Here's the strange thing about monkeys though. They can't live without being fed. So while my, "you're not very pretty monkey" was thrust upon me, I nurtured him and kept him on my back for too many years. My shyness monkey, although I have stabbed him repeatedly, revives himself and tries to climb aboard sometimes, so I'm forced to stab him once again. The important thing is to recognize them and stab them right away. Some monkeys are harder to kill than others. Some monkeys get stabbed and it does little more than tick them off.

I'm a lifelong learner. It's something I'm pretty passionate about. So I'm not kidding when I tell you that I have an entire library of information, self-help, and motivational books and tapes. I love fiction too. So you will often find me engrossed in a book, or more recently reading one on my iPhone, or iPad. Five minutes in the checkout line is time to read part of a chapter. I attend classes and seminars as often as I possibly can. And my car is a classroom with audio CDs crammed in every available space. There is no greater boost to ones self-esteem than learning a new skill, or honing one you already have in your tool belt. I recently attended a public speaking course at Wizard Academy in Austin, Texas. I was humbled to be taught in this class by Roy H. Williams, author of the best-selling *Wizard of Ads Trilogy*, and many other mind-blowing books. I was speaking about Stab the Monkey, when he politely said, "If I stab the monkey, I think I'm just going to have a pissed off monkey. I want to see monkey bits in a blender!" It is a point taken, Mr. Williams.

There are those monkeys that hang on tightly. Sometimes they are the ones we've coddled the longest. The ones that find a way to rename, reinvent, resurrect themselves and reclaim the prime real estate on your shoulders. These are the monkeys that whisper in your ear at every opportunity to keep you stifled, small, and quiet. I urge you to concoct the biggest, baddest blender you can imagine and eviscerate those little suckers. Because I know that you have something to say that needs to be heard. I know that God has implanted in you a seed of greatness. I know this because you're actually reading this book. And that means that you're a learner too. So the next time you tell yourself that you have no time to read, check out how many hours you've spent on Facebook, Candy Crush, or Hay Day. Unless it's to like Stabthemonkey.com on Facebook. That is perfectly acceptable. But that only takes a minute or two. How often do you plop down on the couch and zone out to TV? Did you know that as you watch a stressful situation unfold on TV, your body releases cortisol as though you were actually going through the stress yourself? You're not only wasting time, you're stressing yourself out! Invest in yourself. Learn, grow, read and listen to positive, uplifting speakers. It will pay huge dividends.

I know that someone reading this may say, "You have no idea the tragedy I've been through." Or "You can't even imagine the loss I've suffered." But there are others who do know. There are support groups, and counselors and loving people everywhere who share your pain, and want to help you shed the weight of despair. In today's world of ubiquitous technology, you can find a partner to help you stand and regain your love for life.

What do you want? No, what do you really, really want? It is one of the most important questions you will ever ask yourself. If you don't get very clear about what you want you will never know if you have it. The more clearly you can visualize the image of your life the way you want it to be, the more likely you are to achieve that dream. But now, let's dig a little deeper. Once you've gotten very clear about what you want, ask yourself why. Why do you want these things? No one else will ever look at your answers unless you want them to, so you can be completely honest. For example; if you want a brand new Mercedes, why? If you want to lose 20 pounds, why? If you want a loving relationship, why?

I believe at the very core of most everything we believe we want is happiness. We want things, and relationships and fame and love because we believe it will make us happy. There's another monkey that whispers, "That will make you happy." He's the monkey of lies. Because the real truth is, happiness is within us. We can be at peace and feel joy in the present, with exactly what we already possess. To believe that lying monkey that tells you happiness will come when... is a huge mistake. The sense of accomplishment will come when you achieve a goal, and that will add to your happiness, but you have the ability within you right now to love and appreciate your life and yourself—monkeys and all. I still highly recommend destroying the monkeys. But take just a moment to list some of things you really like about yourself. Write down the things in your life that you are grateful for. Pay attention to the things that bring an easy smile to your face. And make sure to do them more often. Think about how you want to give of yourself to make the world a better place. Think of how you can serve others.

That little exercise just created your goal list. If a monkey starts to say, "You can't do it." Stab him immediately. If he's one of the tough monkeys, stuff him in the blender and push the grind button. You can accomplish your goals. And with persistence, you will achieve your dreams. Every article you read will bring you closer. Every class and seminar you attend will fertilize the seedlings of greatness. Every book, program, and audio that uplifts your thinking will be a catalyst to move you toward your true life purpose. There is so much amazing material available to you. I think of them all as good medicine. Go check out the local library. Try a Google search or YouTube, but stay away from the cat videos! Hours can disappear into cute kitten videos. If you need a good laugh, set a timer and yuck it up. Then get right back to research. Find information on what drives you, and learn all you can about it. The benefits are exponential. Each new thought builds on another until you've reached higher than you dreamed possible.

If you'd like some ideas where to get started, head on over to StabtheMonkey.com and check out my personal reading list. I add to it pretty often. There have been times I attended a seminar, or read a book and didn't get much out of it. But one tiny idea, from an otherwise sub-par event or article can grow into something beautiful for your life. The time and money invested is never wasted. And one more thing I'd like to encourage you to do is share. If you read something great, share it with friends or colleagues. Attitudes are contagious. When you share something uplifting, fun, or beautiful you've brightened the life of someone else. When they share it with others, the light spreads even more. If a butterfly can eventually create a tsunami, then why not start a positive vibration that will rock the world? You can. And I believe you will! ■

Tami Fenton

Tami Fenton is a business owner, writer, speaker, wife and mother. She began her career in radio, earning an award for the best commercial in Texas at the tender age of five. She has enjoyed owning several of her own successful businesses, and helping others to improve both in business and personally. Her passion is to inspire people to become their personal best. Visit her on the web at Stabthemonkey.com

13

Failure to Thrive: Lies We Choose to Believe

By Heather Nichols

"Well, Doctor, what is it?" my mother asked with whimpering concern in her voice, as the doctor held me at arm's length for a moment's examination. In his medical matter-of-factness, he replied in the same tone as any other declaration of diagnosis, "Failure to thrive." After just a few months of life, I was much smaller than expected, not gaining weight or getting the little chubby baby parts that most babies get. And so my mother, having already had my brother two years earlier, recognized something was wrong. Even though the doctor seemed to casually recognize my condition, there was no prognosis or advice given. Thankfully, it didn't turn out to be a serious "condition," but, "failure to thrive" was one of the first words to acknowledge my existence in 1977—and, thankfully, they will not be the last.

Who would have known that as this memory of my mother's was shared with me as a child that this would be just one of several similar negative statements to pillar my life? Although seemingly harmless and insignificant at the time, they would tsunami sadness in my heart, and that big wave would crash, and I would be left to beg that God take my life, as I was not strong enough to take it myself. And he did.

You may be saying, "But, Heather, you're writing this chapter.

So, you didn't die." You're obviously right, but there was a time or two that I was disappointed about that. Hopefully through my story, you too may find encouragement and hope to conquer any gradient of fear, doubt, negative interpretation, sarcasm, victimization, and pursuit of escapism through relationships, sex, drugs, and rock and roll—all the things with which I had "chosen" to fuel my life. And I can assure you: you too are already loved beyond all recognition and built for prosperity.

Like many people, as I've aged and recalled the past years, I see things differently than how I first perceived events in their time. As a young child, I was comforted to hear my mother sing to me, but I was confused by the lyrics. You see, I was "Heather Robyn" on my birth certificate, and my parents decided to call me Robyn. Yet, hearing my mother sing "Walkin' to Missouri," I thought it was a song about me: "Poor little Robyn, a-walkin' walkin' walkin' to Missouri. She can't afford to fly. Poor little Robyn, a-walkin' walkin' walkin' to Missouri, with a teardrop in her eye." The truth was that the song was about "robin," not Robyn. And I grew up never knowing it was a real song by a real group or that it had absolutely nothing to do with me. In my little girl heart, when I heard it, I felt my mom was teasing me. I felt what I imagined the other kids must feel when people poked at them and called them "short." They may be short, but it doesn't help anything to hear it—especially since they can't do anything about it. Nonetheless, I loved my mother, but this song confused me, and the lyrics would continue to trouble me in later years on a bigger scale. In essence, by age four or so, I had already been declared as having physical and financial life challenges. By age four, I say! Well, there is a reason for this, as I will later learn.

Another memory set that created major waves in my life was watching the slow and steady decay of my parents' marriage over the years. There were 33 of those, and I personally saw about 26 of them. Of this span, I feel it's pertinent in my story to relate to you through my heart, again, as a little girl. Whenever yelling between my parents would begin, I'd scramble upstairs to my room. But the Mississippi wood frame house wasn't thick enough to mute the curse words that punched my ears, and the house would tremble when the door slammed. I didn't see my parents spend or make much time for each other, and I remember my dad almost always working. He left when it was dark, and he came home around six. Then he might go work in the yard or someone else's yard. I don't remember him being home much, but when he was, that's when my parents were together, and it became my habit to disappear upstairs…just in case. In fact, when I was about 14, I finally tried to verbalize my discomfort in my own home: I asked my mother, "Mama, why are you and Papa still married?" And that was about the best I had the courage to ask. I secretly wished they would divorce. This experience would affect future relationship choices.

Don't get me wrong, I did feel as though "home" felt like home sometimes, and then there were other times…. Like when I'd be forced to look in the mirror when I was crying while being told, "See what you look like? Now quit crying." This too confused my little girl heart. Another phrase was "Promises are made to be broken." Eh? I thought I understood what that meant at the time, but those words would echo and would add to my bitterness in later years. Again, I knew I was loved, but many times it just didn't feel like love to me. But, in a house of unhealthy communication, how could anything be different? I was just a kid. How would I know anything *should* be different?

Because of the intense emotional dynamics at home, I longed to turn 18 so I could move out. And in junior high, I discovered a temporary option to kind of do that. I heard that another student I admired had recently gotten admitted to the Mississippi School for Mathematics and Science, a kind of college prep school for the gifted. Although the school was exclusively for 11th and 12th grades, students resided on a college campus, and the lifestyle was similar overall.

So I applied, but I didn't apply just to get out of my parents' house. After feeling so much invalidation in my life, I wanted to just be able to say, "See? I did it! I can do something good!" And I heard the local praise and recognition that the other student had gotten for getting accepted to such a prestigious school. Well, lo and behold, I did it too! I got accepted! And I think I got a few accolades. But, most importantly, I was able to say I got in. "Take that, world!"After all that I felt was against me, this was probably the first time I felt approval.

Once my junior year was in full swing at MSMS, instead of finding an escape from my parents, I found a new kind of prison, one of loneliness. I was socially unequipped and made fast friends with a darker crowd. In turn, I learned that some of the most brilliant pre-approved MIT-bound students were also pretty experienced drug users. Thus, I entered into a new community. However, that kind of entertainment only deepened my loneliness, because then it seemed that so many "friendships" were simply woven together just on the common denominator that we liked drugs and some of the same music. In hindsight, there was no satisfaction in that, and still, the unarticulated void in my heart continued.

Next was college. The drugs usage did not lessen, as you could expect, and the stereotypical college life ensued: partying, dating, some studying and more partying. And in one year of my college experience, a strange thing happened. I did finally begin to do less partying, more studying, and more socializing—after meeting "Al." He was a tall, dark, and handsome Venezuelan student with a nice family and position in the local college community. When I was with Al, I got attention, encouragement, respect, and even some laughs. I thought I was in love.

Unfortunately, near time for his graduation, he was rewarded by his uncle with a plane ticket back to Venezuela to visit family. It was during the travel arrangement process that he discovered his visa would be expiring and that his return to Venezuela would become a permanent move. Of course I was torn, and I swore that if neither of us was married by the time I turned 25, I'd come to Venezuela and marry him. Only a couple of years passed with a few emails in between to barely keep us connected, but I eventually arranged a study-abroad to his country.

Al tells me upon my arrival that he's going to introduce me to a friend of his, a Miss Venezuela contestant. She's a drop-dead gorgeous salon owner in town. Tall, thin, pretty, smooth accent and she knows just enough English to have a genuinely polite conversation. No problem. How swanky to have such a friend. Well certainly there should be no contest. I mean, after so much time and heartache, plus a few thousand dollars and a few thousand miles, I definitely deserve to be the winner of any time or affection, right? Wrong. "Ella" was his girlfriend. "Are you kidding me?" I was screaming inside, "All this time and energy and pining away…and THIS??"

It was absolutely devastating for me. I felt incredibly hurt and angry, and I just felt that deep despair—not being able to leave or run away. No, I had to stay and carry out my plan of studying abroad. However, I would do so with an abrupt abhorrence of the thought of "Al" which would last for years to come.

Once back in the States and resuming the more normal college routine, I lived with my parents. The following year, in some seemingly random semi-private moment, my dad looked terribly depressed while telling me he had made a female friend. His facial expressions weren't really matching what he was telling me, and of course I was puzzled. However, the fear of not wanting to cross wires with him and feeling awkward for not knowing the details of what he was referring to changed my response to something generic, like "We all need a friend sometimes." But what I meant was literal, a friend. What he turned out to mean was more than that. Once it occurred to me what he was trying to tell me, I was confused, hurt, and didn't know what to do. I didn't want to be the instigator of something between my parents, and I didn't want to choose sides, and I honestly just didn't want to know any details. Part of me was happier just passing it off as "a phase." And from experience, if my dad was talking, it was the other person's job to just listen. Any response I had given before throughout my childhood was met with invalidation and defense. So, I was reluctant to communicate on any level. My dad's news, however, created a well of anger, which eventually evolved into another huge heartache for me.

Most times in conflict, my "fight" response is much more dominant than the "flight" response. But in this case, I just wanted to run away forever. This was a nightmare come true. The internal conflict it created, the hurt and disappointment, the confusion of what I should do, all of this severely handicapped my ability to concentrate on school—particularly since I was living at home with my parents. I didn't want to look at or talk to my dad. I focused all efforts to entertain myself at friends' houses, and I would fill my schedule with anything I could do to NOT go home.

Finally in despair, and after a couple of months had gone by, I decided that Mississippi should no longer be my home. I wanted to leave the pains of my past behind and completely detach and reinvent myself. So I called my uncle in Texas on a Wednesday, and by that Saturday, I took off in my 1988 Ford Festiva with my clothes and $200 to start my life over. This was 2001.

A fresh and rocky start awaited me in Southlake, Texas. And moving proved to be no cure for problems. It was just a transition into more and various other storms and struggles.

For the first several months, still lonely and prone to fill the holes in my heart myself, I struggled to be socially significant—to family or to anyone. While shooting pool by myself one night, my future ex-husband walked in, saw me, challenged me, lost, and declared a rematch on a date night. And the courtship with "Freddie" began.

Of course, I was very guarded towards dating or relationships on a serious level, based on my recent past. I desired nothing more than a friendship with him, yet he maintained his respect towards me while we had some meaningful conversations. Not getting very romantic but enjoying our friendship, it occurred to me as the saying goes "You should marry your best friend." Still not really knowing what that would look like, although not "in love" with him as he seemed to be with me, he treated me very well and seemed to like the same things I did. He was also overweight but had a cute face. Somehow I found comfort in that, thinking certainly a fat guy couldn't be hard to keep. He was cute, friendly, and likeable by all and seemed to respect me on every level. I considered that maybe this was the "right" relationship to marry into. Not sure, but certain I could make the commitment, I agreed to marry him.

As soon as we said our vows and moved in, everything changed. Freddie instantly became a Dr. Jekyll and Mr. Hyde routine—cute and friendly in public with others, but angry or controlling behind closed doors. I married a nightmare. For six and a half years, I was scolded if I went to the grocery store without him, expected to work my 60-70 hour/week job and clean full time, scolded for buying anything without his approval while he had online spend-a-thons acquiring thousands of dollars of hunting and outdoor equipment (and later discovered $300 cuff links from eBay, and he didn't even have a tux!). And I was told to go cry in a closet because he didn't want to see it. There's obviously much more that doesn't fit into just a chapter. Three Christian marriage counselors later and 99% attendance by only me (all three telling me I should consider divorce), once I decided to, I took steps to divorce as quickly as possible.

We separated in 2009, and I remember the fear that ensued: fear of him coming after me, spying on me, following me…also, fear of the dark, of the quietness of solitude, and just overall fear of my own safety. But, I was willing to face all of these fears for the chance I might still find some purpose for my life. After all the failures and disappointments, I was wondering if there was one.

That next year was frightful. Although I went back to my uncle's house for a couple of months, it was stressful to align employment and living arrangements for a fast transition back to some kind of independence. The most difficult of all was surviving the loneliness. Sure, I was not alone, but I was lonely. I didn't know how or where to find nurturing or comfort for my emotional, mental, spiritual, or financial conditions—all of which were in the mud at the same time. I wouldn't have expected anyone to take me seriously if I had told them, but I recall soaking my pillows for what felt like hours. I cried and whimpered to God like a broken record of huffs and puffs of grief. I prayed he would take my life. At the age of 32, I felt I had worked hard, taken risks, and tried even harder to make good decisions. But, here I was at the cold, dark bottom.

I prayed hard and repetitiously that God would take my life, because I was too weak to take it myself. And in that shaking wet prayer and nearly breathless, it's as though I could hear the Lord answer my question of why in the world was I still here? What was the purpose? He told me nearly instantaneously: I'm still here to tell my story, not that it's really my story, but that it's HIS story through me. And I immediately understood, even without reading it from the Bible, that the Lord wanted me to share my trials and sufferings, that he wanted me to return to obedience, so that it will go well with me and so that He will receive the glory. It became clearer to me that all things really do come together for good for those who are in Christ Jesus. The problem had been that I wasn't in Him; instead, I had been living for myself.

"Oh my pain. Oh my problem. Oh, I'm a victim of this and that. Hardship attacks me." All those sayings were Satan's lies that I had chosen to believe. And the Lord was so patient to still love me through it. I can see now that he was with me all the time, but I was hardened by the "me-disease."

The journey of recovery from such great deception has been and still is incredible. We're told in the Word that we will face all kinds of trials, but we're also encouraged that the Lord will not leave us or forsake us if we continue to follow his guidance. My favorite verse is *Jeremiah 29:11* "For I know the plans I have for you,' declares the Lord, 'plans to prosper you, and not to harm you—plans to give you a hope and a future." Our Lord wants to bless us. And he has already.

No, my problems haven't stopped. I've since been so broke that

I slept on a floor for months, had a bed finally donated to me, had to be fed by food donations for two weeks, was within 24 hours of being homeless but was taken in by someone I didn't know from a local church, and on and on. So the storms of life continue to beat in on me. The difference now is, since the new leaf of my pro-actively seeking God's guidance in every life situation (business, personal, family, communication, wisdom—anything you actually need to know is already in the Bible), that I'm equipped to endure those storms with a much healthier lens. The lies I had previously chosen to believe were: I'm not good enough. I'm a waste of a woman. I'm not worth anything. I have no purpose.... Those lies that Satan had planted through my childhood and young adult years have been replaced with the truth of the word (*Romans 8:1, John 5:24,* and *Jeremiah 29:11*). In fact, we're advised to equip ourselves with the Sword of Truth, and even Jesus had to use scripture himself twice against Satan in the desert. But if we don't know the truth, we can't think it or speak it, so it has to be an intentional act of committing it to memory. We must put arrows into our own quiver. The truth is, I don't need to perform for others: *Galatians 1:10*. When I'm frustrated for not knowing his will for me, the truth is: Romans 12:2.

I now surround myself with the truth. In front of me as I type, I see a plaque with *Philippians 4:8,* "Whatever is noble, right, pure, lovely...think on these things." Thankfully, "Failure to thrive" is now a clear misdiagnosis, according to The Great Physician. Words have such great power. Be careful of the ones you think. ■

Heather Nichols

Some things are normal about Heather's life: she's happily married to Tim Nichols in Rockwall, Texas, participates in Sunday worship and fellowship, watches some good movies from time to time, and procrastinates doing the dishes. Her friends would say she's energetic, tenacious, adventurous, animated, ambitious...But many wouldn't know is that she struggled through depression as a child, suffered tearful stage fright when asked to read aloud in class, escaped emotionally through drugs in her teenage rebellion, has been a victim of sexual violence, had intermittent strokes of academic excellence and "giftedness" (that's what the teachers called it), survived an abusive and controlling marriage, has gone from making lots of money, living on a golf course, and travelling the world to nearly a dozen countries before age 30, to post-divorce having only $200 to restart her life, a no-air conditioned 1985 cracked-leather Mercedes, being socially isolated, sleeping on a floor for six months, being fed by food donations for two weeks, and begging for God to end her life.

In 2011, God didn't take it. Heather gave it. Her relief and fulfillment came NOT from reading the wisdom and guidance of the Word, but doing what it says. She became equipped, and her life since is steadily becoming enriched and satisfying. She is a speaker, marketing consultant, and strategist in her own business called The Biz Fizz, was recently appointed as the Lakepointe Women's Ministry Head Coach in Rockwall, and continues to filter out cultural myths though the ongoing pursuit of truth, success, and contentment in all things. Heather's mission is to edify and fortify other women who may feel they've been a victim of their past or present by educating them on their true value and assuring them of their purpose. For Heather, success is a journey, not a destination.

For speaking engagements, you may contact Heather Nichols at:
thebizfizz.com
genesisters.org
heather@thebizfizz.com
972.590.8908 office
972.896.1576 cell

14

Crossed Roads

By Angie Stone

When people select a profession they usually make a choice based upon what they think they will enjoy doing. We envision what it will be like to fill that role. I am no exception to this way of thinking. I have wanted to be a dental hygienist since my junior year of high school…which was many, many years ago. I saw myself helping people keep their smiles healthy through regular hygiene visits, educating them about dental health and providing oral hygiene instructions. I am sure that these preconceived notions came from watching my own hygienist treat me every six months.

I also had another goal. I just knew I wanted to teach dental hygiene at the college level. That was my ultimate goal. I developed a plan of execution and began paving the road to make it happen. However, somewhere along the line it became clear that my plan and someone else's plan did not really follow the exact same road.

Shortly after I began my hygiene career, my mother in law, Gladys, became so physically ill with Chronic Obstructive Pulmonary Disease (COPD) that she needed to move into a nursing home environment. While she struggled with her illness, I learned many things I never had even thought about. This was my first experience, as an adult, having someone I loved in a nursing home. This, in and of itself, was eye opening and is something we all have the possibility of experiencing, either with a loved one or being there ourselves. It quickly became apparent to me, why people were not all that excited about living in this situation. After all, the food is not what they are accustomed to. The surroundings, no matter how hard the facility tries, are not like their home and they are distanced from those they love. Residents long for a familiar face to walk through their door, just someone to sit and spend a little time with them, someone who understands where they have been and who they once were. I also learned that the care received, while it is the best the employees can absolutely do, is not what I would choose for my mother in law.

However, the reality was that we as a family had no better alternative. We could not take care of her ourselves. One area of care in particular that was lacking beyond belief was the care of her mouth by the care team! Imagine my anguish as a dental hygienist, when I saw periodontal disease (gum disease) get out of control due to inadequate daily oral hygiene assistance and lack of access to a dental hygienist. Yes, it is true that people in nursing homes typically have no access to dental hygiene services, unless there is a dentist who works at the facility, which is not the norm by any means. I had never given much thought about how residents of nursing homes get their teeth cleaned if they can't leave the facility and go to the dental office. Unfortunately, in most situations, they don't!

As Gladys's oral health deteriorated, so did her lung health, or maybe it was vice versa, but the two conditions were definitely related. When the mouth is infected, the bacteria that cause the infection can be easily transferred into the lungs. This can compromise the health of the lungs and result in lung infections such as pneumonia. If you couple this with lungs that do not work well due to COPD, the result can be deadly. Eventually her lung infections occurred closer and closer together. Each infection became harder and harder to resolve. The prescribed antibiotics got stronger and stronger. Eventually nothing more could be done and Gladys lost her life to COPD.

This was heart wrenching for me to watch. I knew that if we could clean up her mouth, the medical team would have better luck clearing her lungs of infection and keeping them clear. At that time, however, I was a new hygienist and was not in the mindset to rock the boat at the nursing home, or risk my license by cleaning her teeth in the facility. So I watched and learned. Upon her death, I vowed to Gladys that I was going to do something so others did not have to endure what Gladys, her care team, family and her dental hygienist had. In all honesty, I had no idea what I was going to do; I just knew I had to do something. After doing research on the situation, it became obvious the only thing I could offer was education to the care teams. Traditional dental visits are not a viable option for most residents due to physical issues, transportation challenges, and money matters. I could not go into facilities and provide dental hygiene services, even though I am a licensed dental hygienist, without the resident seeing a dentist first. This was a huge roadblock for me and the residents. But, teaching the care staff about daily oral care was allowed and while it wasn't the best option, it was something.

Over one summer I educated nursing home care teams in approximately 20 facilities for free. One of these homes was very interested in what I had taught and I quickly developed a relationship with their team. They did have a dentist affiliated with the nursing home, but nothing was set up for providing dental hygiene services. I was able to change that! I gave the facility a proposal which outlined the items I would need them to purchase so I could clean teeth at their facility. They accepted it! I began seeing patients there one afternoon a month. It was a much needed service and I was delighted to be able to get the program up and running.

Even though I was cleaning the teeth of several residents, and was seeing an improvement in their oral health, they still were not as healthy as I had hoped. Something more needed to be done than simply cleaning their teeth every three months. The plaque needed to be controlled more frequently than once every three months. I had been learning about a natural occurring sugar substitute called xylitol. It had been showing amazing dental health benefits in the research. I asked the nursing home if I could do a case study on my own, with a few residents to see if xylitol could help improve their oral health even more. They agreed to a twelve week study. During that time I taught the care team to use xylitol to improve the oral health of the six residents involved in the study. The results were impressive! Xylitol truly helped to reduce the plaque on the teeth and the reduction in plaque resulted in healthier gum tissues. Be that as it may, it still was not as good as it needed to be. I had made great strides, but we could do better.

Meanwhile I continued to practice dental hygiene, and became more and more interested in my senior patients. I had never thought this group of people would bring me so much joy! One patient in particular, Ed, became very special to me. He had been a patient of mine for some 13 years. During this time he came to see me every six months. Initially he walked with the aid of a walker, but as the years passed his physical disability continued to worsen and eventually he could not walk at all. His inability to move on his own, bathe himself or dress himself ultimately landed him in a nursing home. I was saddened by this news when he arrived for his routine hygiene visit, but I knew his independence would be taken from him at some point. My saddened state quickly changed to a horror when I looked in Ed's mouth. What had happened? In my years of treating Ed, I had never seen so much plaque on his teeth and had never seen his gums so red and bleeding.

It was obvious the care he and his wife had been able to perform at home was not being achieved in the facility. Even though he did the best he could to take care of his mouth, his condition had now affected his hands. He was not able to brush effectively. There was nothing I could teach him about brushing and flossing that could turn this situation around. I also knew, based upon my experiences that educating the care team at the facility was not going to improve the brushing and flossing they performed for Ed.

So I took matters into my own hands, literally. I approached my dentist with the following request, "Please write a prescription that states I can go to the nursing home and brush and floss Ed's teeth two times a week and also prescribe two 100% xylitol sweetened mints (1.5g of xylitol) to be administered to Ed after each meal." The reason I asked for a prescription is twofold. One, I was uncertain if I could go and brush and floss without a dentist telling me I could and two, I knew the mints would not get administered by nursing staff without a prescription, even though xylitol mints are available over the counter. The doctor mumbled something about me being crazy, yet he put his pen to the prescription pad. My visits to provide oral care for Ed were very enjoyable! We visited, flossed and brushed, and managed to give each other a hard time now and again.

Before long, Ed's gums were healthy and I began to stretch the time in between my visits. I learned as long as I was there to provide my services once every ten days, his gums did not bleed and the plaque on his teeth was very minimal. During the time Ed was under my care, he was free of dental disease, did not require any treatment from a dentist and never needed emergency dental care.

During Ed's and my time together in the nursing home something special happened. Ed and I became good friends! We were truly good for each other and we looked forward to our visits together. He listened with great enthusiasm to the trials and tribulations of my life and I listened to those of his life gone by. He was instrumental in enrolling some of his fellow residents in a second case study I completed, where I opened up our oral care protocol to 45 other residents. He was my cheerleader, sounding board and advisor.

He was elated when I was asked to present the results of our case study at the International Xylitol Symposium, held in Cancun, Mexico in February, 2013. As a result of the presentation, both of my case studies will be published in a peer reviewed journal! While I was busy working, speaking, writing and seeing Ed, my own grandmother was placed in a nursing home. Unfortunately, I was not able to provide the weekly service for her that I was able to provide for Ed. Since she was able to floss and brush her teeth, and was under the care of the nursing team and the nursing home dentist, I felt she would be okay. She never had troubles with her teeth or gums, so what could go wrong. Well, a lot went wrong.

As her medications increased, her mouth became more and more dry. There are over 400 prescription drugs that cause dry mouth and she was on approximately seven of them. In fact, even though she was legally blind and her body did not work well enough to let her walk, her biggest complaint was her dry mouth! The care team offered what they knew to address the problem, but it was not enough. When there is not enough saliva and bacteria in the mouth are not controlled, teeth get cavities and cavities need to be filled by a dentist. My Gram was on medical assistance. There are very few dentists who take medical assistance for payment of services. As a result, the cavities were not filled. When teeth have cavities that are not filled, they break. As Gram's teeth broke, her oldest daughter would take her out to a private dentist for care...because it now was an emergency. The recommended treatment was always removal of the tooth in question.

This was a vicious cycle, and one that no one, not even the care team or the dentist had any answers to. One day, I received a phone call from my aunt saying that Gram was really concerned with one of her teeth. None of her family or the care team understood how she could have any teeth problems since she had been seen by the nursing home dentist for an exam just three months prior and she was told everything was "A" OK.

I went to see what the trouble might be. What I saw was atrocious!!! There were visible cavities EVERYWHERE! I immediately demanded that my aunt schedule an appointment with the dentist in town to have Gram receive an exam and x-rays, which I paid for myself. His findings confirmed what I had seen. Gram had a cavity in every remaining tooth in her mouth. What I also discovered, after I saw the x-rays, is that in the two short years she spent in that facility, Gram had lost 60% of the teeth she had managed to keep healthy for 90 years. She had become a victim of our broken system of nursing home dental hygiene care.

This is why our elder population has the worst dental health of any population in this country. My Gram, like most other nursing home residents, suffered needlessly from dental disease due to lack of access to a dental hygienist. Once I discovered this, I made it a point to make Gram's dental health a priority of mine. I cleaned her teeth the best I could while she sat in her wheel chair in her room. I made sure that she had things to keep her mouth moist. We switched out her sugared candy for candy sweetened with xylitol. We implemented a xylitol dry mouth spray. Whenever anyone came into her room they would give her a couple squirts of the spray. This ended up being her saving grace! At least her mouth was not as dry. I brushed and flossed her teeth when I went to visit. She always commented how good it felt to have her teeth clean. We were on the right track, at least with her oral care.

As happens to our elders, Gram's body began to shut down. She was getting weaker and weaker, and it was obvious her time on earth was coming to an end. I had been told she was failing, so I immediately went to see her. I could not bear to stay in the room because it was so hard to see her in that condition. She was unable to speak clearly. Her speech was so soft and mumbled that I really could not understand what she said. Seeing her in this state was unbearable. I left the room in tears.

While I was trying to compose myself in the hall my mom came to me and said, "You will not believe what she wants." I was afraid to ask. She wanted me to brush and floss her teeth and give her some dry mouth spray. I honored her wishes. When I was finished she slept. I was with my Gram when she died a few days later. I watched her take her last breaths. The experience will never be forgotten. After she passed, the hospice nurse was going to clean her up before the morgue came for her body and she asked if any of us wanted to be with Gram. I was curious as to what she was going to do, so I watched. I was shocked when the nurse prepared to clean Gram's mouth. Something came over me and I asked if I could do it. As I flossed and brushed Gram's teeth, tears streamed down my face. I could not believe what was happening. When I finished, I gave her some dry mouth spray, kissed her and said good bye. I sent her away with a clean mouth. It would have been important to her. It was the least I could do.

I selected the road of becoming a hygienist. God selected roads that lead me to have a special role as a hygienist. That unlike any other hygienist and He has been persistent. Gladys, Ed, and my Gram were placed in my path for a reason. The journey began with Gladys in 2000 and it is still unfolding in 2013. Every time I let this area of my life go by the wayside, something is placed in my path to refocus my attention here. I had no inkling I would end up loving the elders as I do, advocating for their dental health and making a difference in this fashion. It has become clear. My and God's planned roads have crossed and are lining up to travel together. Thank goodness for these crossed roads! This has been an expedition of watching, listening, learning and finding my passion. It began with a commitment to do something, even though I had no idea what that something was. With God's constant guidance this has turned into something wonderful. Who knows how many people's lives I will be able to make better? You know what? It does not matter. I have been able to improve at least two people's lives and through these experiences my life has been blessed. Greater than all this, is that we all have the ability to make a difference! What are YOU being lead to do? Do you feel God has a different road planned for you? If you do, allow yourself to be led by Him. There is nothing better than when our road and the one He has planned cross. Godspeed. ■

Angie Stone

Angie Stone, RDH, BS has been a dental professional for 30 years. Her professional journey has been anything but ordinary. While working in dental offices she has held the positions of dental assistant, receptionist and clinical dental hygienist. Outside the dental office, she has had articles published in a variety of publications, both dental and medical, and has presented to dental professionals in 35 states and four countries, including Greece, Mexico, Canada and Puerto Rico. She has been a dental hygiene consultant, editor in chief for a dental hygiene publication and a manager of training and education for two companies. Most recently, Angie has been getting the word out that our nursing home residents have extensive oral disease, poor oral hygiene and suffer the worst oral health of any population. She has been working with nursing home facilities and dental hygienists to improve the oral health of this population. It is through this work that Angie promotes the concept, "They shouldn't die of dirty teeth." Angie was awarded the Sunstar Butler Award of Distinction in 2012 for her work with the geriatric population and xylitol, a natural occurring sugar substitute which has been shown to improve oral health.

Angie Stone
www.HyLifeLLC.com

15

Scar Stories and Star Stories

By Charlotte Ann Moore

Then (Jesus) said to Thomas, "Reach your finger here, and look at My hands; and reach your hand here, and put it into My side. Do not be unbelieving, but believing." And Thomas answered and said to Him, "My Lord and my God." *John 20:27-29* NKJV

Like most people my age, I have a few scars on my body. I have some scars from everyday bumps and bruises, and I have some scars from surgery. There is one scar in particular that I rarely think about. I had a large, egg-shaped polyp on my shoulder. It wasn't painful as much as it was noticeable. When people saw me, they thought that I was wearing one shoulder pad!

One pastor tried to pray it away. It didn't help. I tried to ignore it. That didn't help either. Finally, I decided to seek medical attention. The doctor who removed the polyp was a skilled plastic surgeon. After my surgery, the doctor proudly brought me proof of his work: the offending tissue in a glass flask. Using formidable precision, he reattached the skin in such a way that unless you looked closely, you wouldn't notice that I had something wrong with me. All that is left is a very thin scar.

There are some injuries, heart scars I call them, in our lives that are noticeable. They weren't prayed away. They couldn't be ignored. But God, the Master Surgeon, can separate us from the source of our pain in a way that only He can do. The events still happened. The past still occurred. Sometimes we see evidence of what He removed. But the pain is gone. All that is left is a scar to remind you where you came from.

The Old Testament patriarch Jacob had a divine encounter with God. He literally wrestled with an angel. His wrestling forced the hand of the angel. He told the angel, "I will not let you go until you bless me." The angel granted his wish but touched him in the hollow of his thigh. Jacob was left with a limp, but he limped away with a blessing! We may have been hurt by life; we may even be scarred a few times. But there is a blessing that comes from hanging on to God in the tough times.

Incremental Greatness

Sometimes we become discouraged while pursuing our Big Dream because we are looking for the "big win." We keep throwing the life equivalent of a Hail Mary pass. Although those do happen, they happen rarely. We wind up ignoring life's little victories. Those are the ones that really count.

NFL Hall of Famer Emmitt Smith didn't become the NFL leading rusher of all time with big yardage. His solid, stocky body, which caused him to be overlooked by coaches and critics alike, uniquely designed him to do what he did successfully for so many seasons. Sometimes the thing that causes others to pass you over is the one thing that propels you into your destiny. Emmitt Smith was not a flashy runner. He was not known for the dazzling big plays. But he was effective. He achieved greatness one yard at a time.

Greatness, you see, is not measured by the big accomplishments. Greatness is not measured by financial wealth, by notoriety, by power or influence. Rather, greatness is measured in increments. It is measured by the small moments of love that you share on a daily basis. It is measured by the sacrificial gesture. It is measured by how your time is prioritized. It is measured, most of all, by the imprint of your name upon another's heart.

Haters, Waiters, and Gators

Do not be misled: "Bad company corrupts good character." *1 Corinthians 15:33* (NIV)

If you haven't realized it by this point, recognize it now: No Big Dream goes unopposed. There will always be people who don't like what you are attempting to do. Hear me clearly: Don't expect everyone to celebrate you. Not everyone is happy that you want a better life. What if you succeed more than they do? What if you mature, outgrow them and leave their group? Why should you be entitled to success? Besides, you've gotten accustomed to mediocrity and misery; why change now? Every person who is truly committed to change will have critics.

I think that there are three main categories of critics: I call them the Haters, the Waiters, and the Gators. The Haters are well documented. They are the people who appear out of the woodwork as soon as you announce your Big Dream. They are the ones who remind you of all the failed diets, the wasted money and the thwarted attempts. I have a young friend who not long ago announced her plans to have gastric bypass surgery. As soon as she did, some of her own relatives told her she was lazy and crazy for doing so. Against their opposition, she had the surgery. At this writing, she has lost 140 pounds! She made her decision, feels and looks fantastic, and is experiencing a better life. Some people prefer you to be miserable with them than be happy somewhere else.

The Haters are the ones who despise you for daring to dream the Big Dream, for folding the dream into a vision, for mapping out a strategy to achieve it and sticking to the plan no matter how difficult it gets. Haters also show up after you accomplish your Big Dream. They can always find something wrong with what you did.

Here's one way to deal with the Haters: Ignore them. Two men in the Bible were critics of a man named Nehemiah, who was building a great wall for God and His people. One of the men, under the pretense of wanting a friendly dialog, asked Nehemiah to come down from the wall to explain his vision to them. Their ulterior motive was murder. Nehemiah wisely refused the request. Not everyone who smiles in your face is your friend.

The best way to address the Haters is to shine. Focus on your future, not your foes. Some people feed on your adversity like moviegoers with a tub of buttered popcorn. Starve them. You are on your way to becoming a game changer; you don't have time to deal with people who want you on the bench. Nothing succeeds like success.

Too many people want you to waste time explaining your vision to them. You can miss your window of success trying to explain what is in your heart to Haters, who usually don't really care anyway. They just want to murder your Big Dream. Ignore them. Shine around them. And prayerfully avoid them.

The Waiters are more subtle. They don't necessary adopt a public opinion. They wait and see how things turn out in your life. If you do well, they say, "Great! I knew she could do it!" but if you fail, "Well, I never expected him to accomplish much anyway." Sometimes, Waiters come in the form of people who want to hang out with you to waste your time while you are working. Whether they intend to or not, they can be a drain on your time, energy, and emotions.

Address the Waiters in much the same way: with silence and disinformation. Don't talk so much. Seal the leaks in your life. Don't waste time trying to explain your efforts. In the movie *White Men Can't Jump*, one character said that some people would rather look good and lose than look bad and win. Don't be afraid to look bad. Let people assume that your smile hides stupidity. Let them wonder. It's OK if they think it's not going well. The Waiters will know the truth soon enough.

The Gators are similar to the Waiters, but when your job / ministry / business / recovery has barely started, they want to kill it, own it, or distract you from nurturing it. I get the name Gators from the alligators who watch turtles lay their eggs in the sand. Once the egg has been laid, the alligator stealthily makes his way to the sand, digs the egg up, and feasts on something someone else has labored to give birth to.

Like their namesake, Gators function this way largely because it's easier to feed off someone else's resources than to develop their own. Sometimes Gators don't have the desire or ability to start something themselves. Perhaps they don't think you have the right to achieve your vision without their input (in other words, telling you what they think it should look like). They usually don't want to help you while you're working but want to move into your structure once it is built.

There's a book I read during my childhood called *The Little Red Hen*. The hen wanted to bake a loaf of bread. But when she asked for help planting the wheat for the bread, none of the other animals would come to her aid. The harvesting and baking process got the same negative response. But when the aroma of freshly baked bread came wafting through the barnyard, everyone came running.

The Gators are like that. That's why I told you it's important to have your Building Crew around you early in your process, no matter how small the Crew is to begin with. That way, you're less tempted to talk to the wrong people in hopes of gaining support.

Confront the Gators. Put them in check. Like a mama bear guarding her cubs, you have to be passionate about guarding your Big Dream. What God has for you is for you. Do not give it away. I understand that God will protect us. But we have to be careful to guard what He has given us. Guard your hearts.

Beware of people who act as if they believe that for them to be big, you have to be small. Personally, I've fought too hard to be me. I have no interest in giving that up. I'm not talking about being honorable or submissive when appropriate, or not respecting other's opinions. I'm talking about working overtime to please other people so much that you don't even know who you are anymore.

During a memorable ministry conference a few years ago, I

enjoyed a delicious seafood lunch with some pastors. They enthusiastically "got it" when I shared my new ministry vision. The lunch ended with encouragement and prayer for my success. On the way home, I thanked God in prayer for the meeting. He spoke to me, "Do you feel important?" I answered carefully, "No, I feel validated." He responded, "I validated you." It is a point taken. God wants you to get your cues from Him. When you pursue your Big Dream, you will likely have Haters, Waiters, and Gators in your life. But you will be less influenced by them and more affected by Him.

I have wasted so much time waiting for the Haters, Waiters, and Gators to "bless" my efforts. But while I was waiting for them, God was waiting for me! I went from here to there, listening to offers of help, blessing, and covering that never seemed to pan out. All the while God was directing my path and providing me with what I needed when I needed it. Now, my nomadic journey was not wasted at all. God's leading was strategic. He blessed me to be exposed to and participate in various ministry styles and cultures. He also used me to bring diversity, and with the gifts he placed in me, to be a blessing to other churches. I made connections and formed relationships that forever changed my life for the better.

You prepare a table before me in the presence of my enemies. *Psalm 23:5* (NIV)

The Haters, Waiters, and Gators will never completely leave your life. But like using a good room freshener, you can neutralize their influence by dispersing "positive ions" of praise, prayer, and worship. It's not that the "stink" doesn't exist; it just loses its potency in the air. When you focus on what is positive in your life, HWGs lose their power. When the Haters, Waiters, and Gators cannot get a knee-jerk reaction from you with their comments; when you stop allowing yourself to be affected by their toxic behavior; when you start responding instead of reacting, even if they still exist in your life, HWGs will lose their influence over you. Your life will become more of a drama-free zone.

HWG Sandwich

One more thing: When you start to realize your Big Dream, expect Haters, Waiters, and Gators at the next level too. That's because some people at that level are not happy about you making it there. They don't realize that there is more than enough abundance to go around. Some next-level Waiters will watch you scrap, save, and strive as you achieve your Big Dream. Then they may be willing to help you, because they were waiting to see what you did before they reached out. They offer a leg up, not a bailout. We already know what the Gators do. So don't worry about the HWG sandwich. God's got your back.

Purpose Point:

List three Haters, Waiters, and Gators in your life. Think of three ways you can neutralize their influence on you.

The Wall

One goal on my bucket list is to run a marathon. I'm told that when running, you will eventually hit a Wall. That's the point when your knees get wobbly, your legs turn to rubber, and your mouth turns to ashes. Your lungs feel like they are about to explode. Every fiber in your being is telling you to give up. The Wall doesn't happen at the beginning of the race. Not in the middle either. The Wall happens just before the finish line.

There is a point in the pursuit of our Big Dreams when we feel that we absolutely cannot go on. It happens to nearly every one of us. It feels like everything is coming apart. That does not mean that the Big Dream was not real or valid. It means that it's time for you to follow the instructions found in *1 Peter 5:6-7* (NKJV): "Humble yourselves therefore under the mighty hand of God, that He may exalt you in due time. Cast all your care upon Him, for he cares for you." When you humble yourself to God, bringing Him your fears, hurts, and concerns, you put yourself in a position for Him to move supernaturally.

Let me tell you a secret: The Wall usually happens right before your Big Dream breaks through. Then God may give you a second wind to complete your run. Remember, it's not how you start—it's how you finish.

God will break you through your Wall if you press in.

The Rest Stop

We all get tired. It's not surprising; it's expected even. Pursuit of your Big Dream can and will wear you down mentally and physically. Pain can be an indicator of fatigue. Physically, pain helps you to realize that something in your life is not working. It may be time for a quick break in the action.

It's OK at times to rest. Find a safe place to nurture your body and your spirit. By now, you should have made your home your haven. Go to your Rest Stop and take care of you. Keep healthy foods in stock for the times of fatigue and exhaustion. This is no time to overload on the carbs, the sugar, and the caffeine. Of course, I personally think dark chocolate is OK...

Have an alternative Rest Stop outside your home (one that is Hater, Waiter, and Gator-free). Maybe it's a good friend's house or your favorite Starbucks during their downtime. Ask someone on your Building Crew if you can stop by occasionally and grab a sandwich, rest, and get some encouragement.

But don't lose heart if you can't find a Rest Stop. Sometimes you can't find a friend. But you can always find a friend in God. At one point in his reign, even King David had to encourage himself when his entire army abandoned him.

Whether encouraged by yourself, your friends, or the Word, don't apologize to anyone for needing a Rest Stop. There are no superheroes in the cemetery. Take time to rest, to recover, to pray, to meditate, to read your Bible, and to regroup.

Power Point

Schedule ONE hour out of your day this week and do... absolutely nothing.

Playing with Pain

I love watching the number one golfer in the world, Tiger Woods. I don't know a thing about golf, but I know a relentless competitor when I see one. Tiger's will to win is unparalleled. Out of his (current) 14 major wins, his 2008 U.S. Open win was phenomenal. To win the tournament in sudden death overtime, with an injured leg! Have you heard of an "ugly win"? Some wins are not pretty—but a win is a win.

The greatness we talked about earlier doesn't just belong to the Tiger Woods and Dirk Nowitzkis of this world. It belongs to everyone who makes the decision to keep coming back. We may have to play with pain at times. We may have to attempt victory with one leg. Your win may not be pretty, easy, or applauded by everyone in your life. But that makes your victories that much sweeter. When you find yourself playing with pain, this is a time to dig deeper, elevate your game, and press on.

Star Stories

Star stories happen after you focus on the blessing and not the bitterness, when God has brought you through situations that have driven others to suicide, though you may be broken, bruised, and battered. As He heals you of your issues, you will, I promise you, be able to look back over your life and be thankful for the peaks and the valleys. You will have extracted the purpose from your pain and come through with power. Through the miracle of a touch from God and time, "scar stories" will turn into "star stories."

Like the external scar I told you about in the beginning, I have heart scars too. But now, most of them don't hurt anymore. Now I can share my star stories with others without reliving the pain that produced the scar in the first place.

A Prayer for You

Father, like Your Son's scars, our scars are a testimony. Thank you for the visual and not-so-visual reminders of Your power, love and grace. Help us to deal with the Haters, Waiters and Gators—the ones we know about and the ones we don't see. Help us to march towards greatness one yard at a time. Most of all, thank You for taking us through our pain and not leaving us in it. In Your Son's Name, Amen.

Reflective Questions

What little victories can you encourage yourself with?

How do you neutralize the Haters, Waiters, and Gators in your life?

Do you have a safe Rest Stop for when you are physically, emotionally, and spiritually exhausted?

What is your strategy for responding when you hit the Wall?

What Scar Stories and Star Stories is the world waiting to hear from you? ■

Charlotte Ann Moore

Charlotte Ann Moore is a writer, speaker, ordained minister and an advocate for creative wellness. She is the author of more than 100 business, technical, travel, inspirational and motivational articles.

Her purpose and passion is to inform, encourage, motivate and inspire people first to discover then walk into their purpose and destiny.

Charlotte Ann is a graduate of Southern Methodist University. Her interests include coffee, people, WordPress, writing, and beginning guitar. Connect with her at CharlotteAnnMoore.com.

16

How One Life Can Impact Many

By Bill Williams

At age 17, I entered the Explorer Olympics at the Millington Naval Base near my home in Memphis, Tennessee. I won two medals, gold in Obstacle Course and silver in Diving. Although I was already an Eagle Scout and had received the Order of the Arrow, this Olympic event was a foreshadowing of what would become a recurring theme in my life: seeking help from someone who knew more than me and overcoming obstacles put in front of me.

The diving medal signified the "springboard" that was used to launch into something new. Springboards are like mentors who propel you into space in order to reach new heights. I have lived my life going from one mentor to another and have become a mentor to others as a result. I am a firm believer in The Word and in *Proverbs 27:17* which says, "As iron sharpens iron, so one person sharpens another."

The obstacle course gold medal speaks to overcoming challenges no matter how daunting they seem. We were competing on a military base where marines prepared for battle. We had to go over, around and through physically tough barriers to reach the end of the timed obstacle course. Being quick, nimble and strong were the attributes that led to my success. Over the years, I overcame a speech impediment to become an international speaker, a coach and leader of one of the top dental practices in America.

Charlie "Tremendous" Jones favorite quote was taught to me by Dr. Ron McConnell of Quest, a dental management firm, in 1981. "Where you are a year from now will largely depend on the books you've read and the people you've met." Books and people have played a pivotal role in my life; it happened early and often...and continues to this day. Ron taught me that it was possible to break free from others and my own self-imposed expectations. To succeed is to stand on the shoulders of giants: the teachers, mentors, saints and team members who supported you all along the way.

Mentors Are Springboards

The first dental springboards in my life were Dr. Harold Gelb and Dr. Bernard Jankelson. They taught me about TMJ and the orthopedic and the neuromuscular position of the jaw related to the head. This allowed me to gain a much broader view of head and neck pain, dental occlusion and TMJ than was taught in my doctoral training program. It opened the doors to becoming an international lecturer on the subject. Combining those techniques with the teaching on myofascial trigger points which I learned from Dr. Janet Travell, President Kennedy's personal physician, I have treated pain patients with amazing success for the past 35 years. They dared to be different, to break free from the dogma of the "so-called experts" of their day and viewed the patients in a whole new, scientifically valid light. Because of my choice of mentors, my path took a completely different direction than that of most my classmates at the Medical College of Georgia. We now treat head and neck pain as well as regular dental patients from all over the world as a result.

Engagement

Dr. Justin Jones formed the Atlanta Craniomandibular Society with me and nine other dentists in 1979. He was our mentor and we met monthly for over a decade advancing our knowledge of neuromuscular dentistry. While meeting in his office, he demonstrated how he treated patients. We learned his unique methods of chronic pain management, TMJ treatment and orthodontics. His value to us was in how he synthesized the work of Gelb, Jankelson, Rocobado, Bell, Witzig and Farrar into a philosophy from which we in turn created a system...the Framework Orthopedic System (FOS). Dr. Larry Tilley and I taught the FOS to thousands of dentists over the next three decades. Dr. Justin Jones took the time to gather a small group of open-minded dentists and the rest was history. Investing time with individuals pays the largest dividends. There is no substitute for engagement. Making a difference in someone's life changes the course of history. When my first son was born, Sheila, my wife, and I decided to name him after Dr. Justin Jones because he dared to be a difference maker.

There are four seasons to a dentist's life, much like the seasons of the year. In the spring of my career, I focused on the didactic, the technical information to become competent...a good dentist. You saw how the association with those select mentors I mentioned above launched my career into a TMJ, orthodontic and reconstruction direction. The summer, or expansion phase of my career, the period from 1985-1995, was heavily influenced by Dr. Omer K. Reed of Phoenix, AZ.

Balance

Omer taught me to value the Balance of Life concept of living and his famous quote that I learned to live by was, "If it's been done, it's probably possible". At this time, I began to set mentors before me for all of life's goals and needs, not just dentistry. I began to value the coach, the consultant, the counselor in my life. Omer was good in teaching word formulas and equations such as NASTE. In order to sell anybody anything first you have to cover Need, Answer, Source, Time and Economics (cost)...NASTE. Just find out what the problem is, identify the solution, show them you are the one to deliver that solution and finally figure out when is the right time and proper cost so that both parties feel good about the result.

Omer was good at getting others to set lofty goals and finding someone to help you get there. He held, at his home in Phoenix, a workshop called The Million Dollar Roundtable: The Anatomy of the Accelerated Practice. In 1987, I set a goal to be a presenter at that Roundtable. I had never produced a million dollars in my practice before in a single year, yet by the time I spoke at the workshop in 1989, we had. Overcoming the seemingly insurmountable obstacle of something like producing a million dollars in one year was actually possible when viewed as only having to produce $5,000 a day, working a normal 200 days a year. The key was systems and consistency.

If we are to have an impact in people's lives, we have to touch them. We have to get below the surface and meet them where they are, where they live. You have to go to them. I remember on one occasion Omer picked Sheila, my wife, and I up at the Phoenix airport himself. He served as he wished to be served. Another time, I hosted him in Atlanta at Emory University School of Dentistry and then later in our back yard on the deck next to the pool for our private dental study club, the Solstice Group.

I like to tell this story about Omer in our backyard. While lecturing to our group, standing in the yard on the grass, Omer spots a ball. It's bright blue, a marbled color, approximately 10 inches across. He casually takes aim and playfully kicks the beach ball... but it only goes three or four feet from the original spot where his foot impacted it above the grass. The "beach ball" was in reality a bowling ball yet Omer did not miss a beat. He carried on his lecture, stoic and unflinching. Back at the Million Dollar Roundtable six months later, I was happy to make a presentation to Omer, to his surprise...again. We cut that bowling ball in half, mounted it on a wooden plaque with the engraved brass plate reading, "To Our Leader and Mentor Dr. Omer Reed—Things May Not Always Be What They Seem". When surprises and challenges come into our life unexpectedly, do you keep your focus and composure like

Omer?

The Harvest

Autumn or the fall season follows summer and that was true for me as well. After a season of growth, must come the season of harvest. Don't forget to plan for the harvest. Don't forget to store up what you harvest. Those words are full of irony in my life because I have had the opportunity to go through two harvest seasons, having survived my winter of discontent, that time of utter failure and been reborn in a number of ways, out of the ashes like the phoenix rising from the ashes in ancient Greek mythology.

You see, from the time I sold my dental practice in 1993 to 1997, two bad things happened. One, I had to take it back because the buyer dentist got into some personal problems and because I had self-financed the sale, I had to resume running the practice. Two, most all of the money I had in my savings and retirement plan was lost because of bad investments during that same time. And the stock market meltdown over the dotcom bust was about to take the rest very soon. We sold our practice in Stone Mountain for a song just to get away from a deteriorating neighborhood. My wife and I started over at age 48 at just about the same place we had been 23 years earlier, except that we now had two boys in high school about to attend college.

Bob Buford wrote an outstanding book called *Halftime*. I identify with his message and call the period between 1997 and 2001 the "halftime" in my life and my career. I found my purpose; I found my cause. I reconnected with my wife and my family. The things that matter were illuminated and the follies of the past were set aside. For 23 years, I had been building on my own understanding of the way things should be, following the mentors and reading the books, but doing it my way with my focus on myself.

Be a Good Listener

Sheila, my wife, was my mentor during this period which was the new spring time of our life. She suggested that we pray about where to relocate. We decided to let go and let God become the center of our lives, not just in helping us as to where we should start a new dental practice. Planning would always include Him as we prayed for guidance and to be led by the spirit instead of just our own thoughts and understanding. One piece after another began to fall into place, the signs of where we were to relocate and set up practice became abundantly clear. We had searched each and every community from Cumming to Covington for the ideal dental practice location, surveying every major crossroad.

While in north Gwinnett on Suwanee Dam Road, we turned into a dirt road and promptly got our Jeep's back wheel stuck in a ditch. Within a minute a truck showed up, stopped, and the man asked if he could help us. We said yes, thank you, and he proceeded to pull out a big chain and pull us out of the hole we had gotten ourselves into. We later called him our Suwanee guardian angel. Then, there was our old friend at Atlanta Dental Supply, Dean Cox, who had helped me find my first practice location in Decatur 23 years earlier. He called a week after the ditch incident to say there was an abandoned dental office in Suwanee for lease. Within a month of meeting our "angel" we had signed a lease in Suwanee and the beginning of a wonderful relationship with a new community began.

The wisdom of listening to my wife when she suggested we pray about where to go and to look for God to lead us was the treasure at the end of my 23-year "first" career. Listening to the Holy Spirit has made a tremendous difference on our "second" career, as you are soon to learn. After all, He is our counselor and the best mentor one could ask for.

Belong To the Community

One reason we would become successful so rapidly in our new location, Suwanee, GA, was because we worked to become knitted into the fabric of the community. Sheila and I moved with our two sons, Justin and Tyler, who were 9th and 11th graders in high school, to within five minutes of the office. We loved the commute and more importantly we were living near our patient base. We got to interact with them on a daily basis, joining the North Gwinnett Football team sponsors, attending the local church, Sugar Hill UMC, belonging to the Suwanee PowerCore networking group, being a member of the Gwinnett Chamber of Commerce and its Chairman's Club. Showing up is 50% of success.

Operate From a Vision

Without a yellow page ad, our presence in Suwanee would have been unknown unless we did something out of the ordinary. Since the Internet has just recently been popularized and web sites the new rage, I became webmaster of my own web site in 1998. I developed a concept called Web-Centric Marketing and pointed all of my marketing activities back to the home page of SuwaneeDental.com. This became the centerpiece of our growth that averaged a $500,000 increase each year for the next ten years. Having a marketing action plan, and implementing it, will spur growth and lead to any business's success. "Where there is no vision, the people perish…" is *Proverbs 29:18*. Having a vision, mission and purpose, all help you to focus on the task ahead. Part of the development of our life balance plan was to implement our vision and mission as a holistic action, not one just focused on our dental business. Take a look at what our written practice vision and mission have been for the past decade.

Vision Statement

"To create smiles people love throughout the Southeastern USA with comprehensive, comfortable, state-of-the-art dentistry and… To offer love, hope and light to seekers in all nations through dental mission experiences."

Mission Statement

To glorify God by being the best dental practice in Georgia by…

- Delivering quality and excellent dentistry in a timely manner to discriminating individuals

- Keeping up-to-date with our continuing education and state-of-the-art equipment
- Creating a home-like practice environment that both staff and patients love
- Addressing the needs of local and international groups in need through dental missions
- Providing a rewarding career to career-minded dental professionals
- Listening to the needs and wishes of patients of all ages, backgrounds, and socio-economic status
- Offering comprehensive, comfortable, complete dentistry to all patients
- Mentoring with our team to allow each member to become fully trained, competent and able to handle the expectations of their fellow team members.

As you can see, we are patient centered, team driven and driven by the faith and belief that there is a God who loves us and who wants us to treat His people as we would like to be treated. We follow the Golden Rule in our practice and strive to be the best practice under the sun. We firmly believe that God rewards those who choose to follow Him, invest in working diligently with what He has given them, and who are out in the fields spreading the Good News, planting seeds and helping with the harvest.

The Turnaround

So, how did I come to this point in my career, after 23 years of practice, where I was actually seeking God's will for my life and applying Biblical principles to my business? It can all be traced back to mentors and challenges, once again. Here's the short version…

Sheila, my wife and mentor, was a discussion leader for Bible Study Fellowship. She had asked me to go and take the classes for several years because it was so good. I knew it was good but did not want to commit to the rigor of the study…weekly sessions with homework to complete. But, for Christmas in 1999 she asked me to give her one thing: go to the Intro Class for Bible Study Fellowship (BSF). I figured, no problem, I liked classes, and would just go and see what it was all about. Needless to say, I opted in and the rest is history. I took ten years of classes, every Monday night of the school year and even became a discussion leader myself. It was the most important growth aspect of my Christian life and where I truly learned what God intended for me to know about Him. I finally understood Jesus' teachings and I found my purpose somewhere along the way.

Africa

In 1999, my brother, Brad Williams, a pastor in the North Georgia Conference of the United Methodist Church in Social Circle, GA, went to Kenya on an evangelism mission trip, showing the Jesus film to the Masai and Kipsigese tribes in Swahili. A little girl named Mercy, badly burned, caught him and his family's attention. They saw the need for medical help in that remote village. She was the one; it was her need that launched a mission. Brad came back and announced that he was going to build a medical clinic in Olmekenyu, Kenya and needed help. So, on my 50th birthday, April 9, 1950 we held a birthday party / fundraiser for Kenya Medical Outreach. With the help of many, particularly Millard Bowen and Virgil Williams, we raised a good sum to build the clinic and that year, Brad and Millard took a team of 20 Atlanta-based builders to construct the clinic. It all started from a vision and a desire to help.

When Mercy Clinic was ready to house patients, in May of 2001, we took our first mission trip to Kenya. Eight of us worked from 8:00 a.m. to 11:00 p.m. treating dental patients in the daytime and showing the Jesus film in remote villages at night. We would travel by four-wheel Land Rover over barely passable dirt roads to crank up the gas generator and power up the VCR to show the movie to people who had never seen a movie or heard the story of Jesus in their life. It was an adventure that we would do annually for the next 11 years and expanded into medical and veterinary clinics, building community buildings, churches, water projects, silos for grain, schools, feeding the hungry, supporting pastors, training nurses, teaching classes and holding Tembae Na Yesu (Walk To Emmaus) spiritual development weekends. All this happened because we said yes when called...and the practice continued to flourish.

Bold men said yes; they dared to make a difference. Working with Brad, Millard, Virgil, Sheila, Geofrey Githuka, our faithful driver, John Leshoe, the Masai village leader, Dr. Daniel Chepyegon, our local dentist in Narok, Kenya, Dollie Sauls and Penny Martin, our short-term missionaries turned long-term resident missionaries, Dr. Jon and Lisa Bird, RN ,Cheney Davis LFP who staffed the medical clinic along with Pam Smith RN, Mike and Lisa Derrick, Lisa Stamper, and Hayden Norman pioneered the Tembae Na Yesu with Brad and Sheila, my sons, Tyler and Justin Williams, Luke Ellington, Charles Ellington, Jerry Loughery and a host of others, we made a big difference for our brothers and sisters in Kenya. As the district commissioner told us on our second trip back to Olmekenyu, "You made a difference in the people. They had felt forgotten, even by their own government. You gave them hope!"

Epilogue

It's been 38 years since I opened my doors to treat my first dental patient. Sheila and I are working just as hard as ever. We've faced those challenges that come at us around every corner. We recognized our springboards and used them to find solutions to those challenges. I sold the practice and am now the Senior Managing Dentist at Suwanee Dental Care instead of the owner. I still love being a dentist. But, remember, everyone needs to plan their transition. We have a fine consulting and coaching business, Solstice Dental Advisors, which helps dentists all across the USA and Canada. Yes, mentors are still a part of our lives as we enjoy being mentors to others. We find that the secret is to engage and take action, not just plan and plan and plan. In 2011, we founded Glory

City Church along with our good friends Tom and Donna Wilson and Pastor Tony and Kathy Thompson. Balance and vision are two key ingredients we are teaching our herd. Life is good and the springboard to our next adventure is just one challenge away. ■

Bill Williams

Dr. Bill Williams is a highly acclaimed practicing dentist and an expert in neuromuscular, TMJ, cosmetic, laser and implant dentistry as well as dental marketing and management. During his 25+ years of practice, he has built several group dental practices.

His consultancy, Solstice Dental Advisors, equips dentists by implementing strategies to grow and improve their practices. Over his career, he has been featured at Dr. Omer Reed's Napili VIII: The Million Dollar Roundtable, lectured for Quest Seminars, Myotronics, Bioresearch, the annual meeting of the Academy of General Dentistry, international conferences of the International College of Craniomandibular Orthopedics in Japan, Canada and Italy, was Senior TMJ Instructor for the United States Dental Institute and was a co-founder of TMJ Framework, a mini-residency for head, neck and facial pain.

He was named the Small Business Person of Year in Gwinnett, was the recipient of the Ron Lamb Award from the Christian Dental Society and is the co-founder and director of Kenya Medical Outreach, Inc. Dr. Williams is an author, clinician, teacher and mentor in addition to managing Suwanee Dental Care. He and his wife are pastors of Glory City Church Atlanta.

For more information, go to: SolsticeDentalAdvisors.com and Suwanee-Dental.com.

Dr. Bill Williams, DMD, MAGD, MICCMO
Solstice Dental Advisors
400 Peachtree Industrial Blvd 5-299
Suwanee, GA 30024
solsticedentaladvisors.com
770-614-4249 (office)
678-858-3381 (cell)

17

Because My Mother Taught Me

By Chris Brady

I was raised in Manassa which is a small Colorado farming town. For you older folks, Jack Dempsey, the world champion heavyweight boxer was born there. He was known as the Manassa Mauler. The town was one mile square. No stoplights. One restaurant. One gas station. One grocery store. 2 churches. Lots of mosquitos.

I grew up milking a cow twice each day-no matter what. I rode a horse to drive the cattle up to the mountains for summer pasture. I also cut hay and grain-beer barley for Coors.

And we had challenges as a family. Money was scarce. My dad would borrow money (working capital) in the spring to help with planting and harvesting the crops and getting the cows to the mountains. In the fall, we'd sell the calves and pay off the loan to the bank. Then, it was 'Rinse. Repeat' in the spring.

My mother would put iron-on patches on my jeans. There were lots of hand-me-downs. We shopped from catalogues. (Again for you younger folks, that was how we shopped from home before there was the Internet.)

Most of the time I had to work instead of going to summer camps close to a big city. I thought I was picked on at the time. It was cold in the winters...very cold. We often had to work outside. My eyelids would freeze shut in the -40 degree weather. I remember my dad making me chase a cow in a 40-acre field that was ready to give birth. She did not want to go into the barn. I don't know how cold it was but there was snow on the ground and I had only a sweater and what we used to call 'Sunday shoes'—shoes that I would wear to church. Boy was I mad at him. At the time, I could have cared less if the newborn calf froze. I was freezing!

There were very few resources to improve our talents. No fancy high school music program. No elaborate fitness equipment for sports. No so-called 'experts' to guide us to the next level of expertise. But…in spite of all this, I grew up to be what many people would call successful.

Now, I don't want you to feel sorry for me. Because everyone in the town was pretty much in the same boat, I thought everything was great. Now that I'm grown, I realize that how I was raised ended up being a blessing in almost every way. As cliché as it sounds, the challenges made me stronger. In fact, as odd as it might seem, my wife would move to Manassa in a minute if we could make things work professionally. We both love the people. They are hardworking, down-to-earth, honest and willing to help when you're in trouble.

This is where it gets hard for me to write. Simply because, it sounds like I'm bragging about myself and providing a resume of all the things that I've accomplished. Please know that the only reason I'm sharing this with you is NOT to make myself look great, but rather to show you what can happen to a young man when his mother teaches him the correct principles.

A few years ago, I returned to Manassa for my class reunion. (Because we consolidated with other small towns in our valley, we had a class of 106 people.) It was great to see everyone. Something that was very important to me was when we shared with each other the details of our lives. I was the only one who had an advanced education. Many were struggling financially. Many had lost their teeth. Some were alcoholics. But as we talked, something became very apparent to me. Most of my classmates were looking at me like I was some sort of celebrity. I wasn't sure how to feel about that. Maybe I was embarrassed?

That night, I went home, pondering about what had happened in my life that would allow me to have the blessing of growth and prosperity that my fellow mates had not experienced. After analyzing events that had propelled me forward, the answer came loud and clear. *It was because my mother taught me.*

That hit me like a ton of bricks. So, what did my mother teach me? It's really quite simple. I'll share that with you later but let me first tell you what my life was like to see if you can identify how it all happened.

When I was eight years old, my mom drove me to the orthodontist whose office was over two and half hours one way. She somehow knew that having straight teeth would be important in my life and was willing to make the sacrifice not only financially but also with her time. She had 5 kids! She taught piano lessons to pay for any "extras".

It was during those years of wearing braces that I decided that I wanted to be a dentist. I liked the fact that a dentist didn't have to work outdoors. It was always the same temperature. And, he had weekends off to be with his family, etc. My mom gave me the confidence that I could do that.

Soon after that, I told her that I wanted to take guitar lessons. Again, she taught piano lessons to make that happen. I started out with a borrowed guitar that was old and cracked. After a few months, my teacher recommended a beautiful guitar in the music store. But, it was $150 and my dad told me that we didn't have the money for it. A couple of weeks later, I came home from school. Both mom and dad were waiting for me. They had smirks on their faces. My dad quickly asked me if I would like to go play basketball. I loved to play basketball with my dad and so I jumped at the chance. We had a small storage area underneath the stairs where we kept the basketball. He asked me if I would get the ball and his shoes he stored under the stairs. I jumped up and went to get the ball. When I opened the door, there was a big bag on top of the basketball. I moved the bag to get the ball and as I did so, I noticed that the bag had something in it that was a very familiar shape. My heart raced. I grabbed the bag, opened it and found a shiny, new guitar from the music store. I couldn't believe it. My parents had tears in their eyes. I was so humbled because I knew how much of a sacrifice it was for them.

Mom encouraged me to sing and play my guitar. She always said to me. "Chris, you can do anything you want." Over the years she repeated to me how well I could sing. In high school, I was asked to sing frequently including at my high school graduation. Mom told me that I was smart. She helped me learn how to read very well. I was awarded several academic honors. She helped me understand my value. I was voted the student "Most Likely to Succeed". I was the district pole vault champion. I got 6th in the state meet simply because my teammate failed to catch my pole and it knocked the bar off. My teammate ended up getting the fifth place medal instead of me. You can tell that I haven't totally forgiven him. My fellow students voted me student body president. My mom told me that I was probably the best president the school had ever seen.

College I got an academic scholarship to BYU which was a very large university filled with enormous talent. Not too many of those in Manassa. I got on the pre-dental academic track. When I got to BYU, my sister-in-law told me about auditions for a singing group (Young Ambassadors) that traveled all over the world. I said to myself that my Mom told me that I was 'the best' singer she had ever heard so I grabbed my guitar and headed for the auditions. As I walked into the room, I watched the other auditions for a brief moment. The talent blew me away. There were people who sang on television for cartoons and other shows. I was very intimidated. "We're not in Manassa anymore." I wanted to click my red slippers and leave. When it was my turn, I slowly walked to the front of the room. I watched the judges, trying to read their thoughts, but I had no insight to what was going on in their heads.

The next day, I went to see if I had made callbacks. Nope. Didn't even make the first cut. I was devastated. Had my mother been lying to me?

That afternoon, I received a phone call from the director from another entertaining group (The Sunshine Express) who said that she saw my audition and was interested in hearing me sing again. Long story short, I made that group. She told me that the director of Young Ambassadors wanted me to get some more experience and Sunshine Express was the ticket.

After that year, I:

- Was chosen to sing with the Young Ambassadors. The pinnacle of my singing career was when I was selected as the top tenor in the Western United States to be part of the All-American College Singers. Over 5,000 college students from across the nation auditioned. I sang Happy 50th Birthday to Mickey Mouse on the Space Stage in Disneyland five times each day and rode a float singing (actually lip sinking) in the pre-parade to entertain the guests who were waiting for the electric light parade to begin.
- Graduated from BYU in three years.
- Was accepted to and graduated from Baylor College of Dentistry.
- Practiced dentistry for 10 years, and then…
- Started my own dental consulting and coaching business.

20 years later, I'm still coaching dentists and their team across the United States. I have been voted the top dental speaker at one of the most prestigious dental conferences in the world—The American Academy of Cosmetic Dentistry. I have spoken to thousands of dentists sharing my message of "Practicing from the Heart". It's been good to me. More importantly, I have not only changed many dental offices for the better, but because of what my mother taught me, lives have been changed.

As I said earlier, I hope that the above does not make you gag.

I hoped to portray to you how one person can have a positive effect on another person with the right message. That is a message of truth.

What did my mother teach me? What was the foundation of my success? What and how was this great motivation created? It's very simple. She taught me truth. She taught me from her heart. She taught me that I was of Infinite Worth. She taught me that no matter what, I could always come out on top. She taught me to believe that I could do anything…that I was the best. And even if I didn't think that about myself, I could always dig deep and remember that my mother knew it and believed in me.

There is one other critical piece of importance. This is not a 'rah', 'rah', positive mental attitude sort of thing. It's not about positive self-talk. It doesn't require meditation. No phony rhetoric. No surface enthusiasm. That's not how she is. She's quiet and unassuming. But when I say she taught me truth—that I was of Infinite Worth—she knew it with her entire soul and I believed it.

Because my mother taught me, I was able to overcome. Just overcome. Thank you, Mom. You're the best. You are of Infinite Worth. ■

Chris Brady

Dr. Chris loves helping dentists produce large amounts of whatever it is they want in dentistry and in life. Happiness. Family time. Time off. Financial Freedom.

For two decades, he has taught principles and concepts that have changed the lives of literally thousands of people in the dental profession.

Listening to Dr. Brady you'll find yourself laughing at yourself and even feeling a bit embarrassed at some of the crazy things we naively do and say to patients.

Most of all, Dr. Brady is a genuine, generous person eager to share his message.

Dr. Brady received his B.S. degree from BYU and is a 1984 graduate of the Baylor College of Dentistry. He resides in Colorado Springs. He is most famous for having eight children and one wife—and he sang 'Happy 50th Birthday' to Mickey Mouse everyday for an entire summer on the Space Stage in Disneyland

Dr. Chris Brady
richdentistseminars.com
drchris@bradygroupllc.com
1-888-292-7239

18

Don't Give Up, Get Up

By Heather O'Brien Walker

I was ecstatic about figuring out all the details for my upcoming wedding and at the same time I was jumping in with both feet into a new position as an executive at a luxury retailer. There was a lot going on but I was very excited about everything that was in store for me. I couldn't have been happier…I was at the top of my game, until one fateful day in July.

On the afternoon of July 29, 2011, I was going about my typical day as a new executive. I was overseeing a staff of 30 cosmetics consultants, over 50 vendors and millions of dollars in product. I was busy to say the least! I had recently finished a project that had me traveling the world as a global hospitality consultant that took me from Germany to Tahiti and everywhere in between.

I was ready to settle down after that year abroad, had returned to Florida, and to my new position. A few months before, I had met the man of my dreams on an online dating site. He was the tall, dark and handsome type that I had been looking for: my own Cary Grant with a wicked sense of humor. While accompanying him on a business trip, overlooking the majesty of the breathtaking Grand Canyon, he had asked me to marry him. I accepted without hesitation. I was overjoyed to think that I would be spending the rest of my life with him.

I had been through many experiences at this point in my life that had tested my perseverance and my ability to overcome tough challenges. I had learned from these experiences to choose a mantra that I always told myself in trying times where I seemed knocked down and flat on my back, "Don't Give Up, Get Up!" I also learned about the art of visualization. Those two tools became two of the most important things that made a difference in the outcome of any challenging situation that I faced. I know that many people speak about positive self talk or mantras and visualization, but few have elevated it to an effective art form.

The first time that I ever heard about the art of positive self talk and visualization was from Jack Canfield in the film *The Secret*. I was glued to the screen when he told his story of how this strategy had worked for him so brilliantly and the success it had brought him. I was hooked. But how would I create effective visuals? I choose to take the knowledge from Mr. Canfield and marry it with my experience in Hollywood.

Earlier in my career I had been fortunate to work among some of Hollywood's greatest stars including Bruce Willis, Patrick Swayze, Tom Cruise, Drew Barrymore, Mike Myers, Elizabeth Taylor and Demi Moore to name a few. The film making community is masterful at creating compelling images that seem to pull you into another world. The power of the visual images flickering across the screen can take you on an emotional journey that can literally change the way you look at life, so I decided to create my own "mind movies" with a positive self talk score. Over the years they had been very effective for me in overcoming obstacles.

I had no idea that choosing to make my "mind movies" would become vital to my very survival.... That July day in 2011, my life would be forever altered. The events began to unfold as I was making my way to my office after leaving a meeting with the other store executives. Everyone was thrilled with my progress over the short time that I had been there. I was riding high with all the accolades and was really feeling at home with my co-workers and staff. I was looking forward to meeting my girlfriend after work to go over wedding ideas and hone in on my dress. That meeting never took place.

What do you think the odds are of sustaining two brain injuries within 40 days? That's just what happened to me on July 29th, 2011. I assure you, I wasn't jumping out of airplanes or living in a war zone or playing a professional contact sport…I was just like you. Instead of going through my usual work day, I fell over a cardboard box filled with trash that someone had left carelessly in a stockroom walkway. I fell violently forward striking the front of my head first on a heavy metal shelf, knocking me unconscious, and then again striking my head as I fell face first onto the concrete floor.

No one knows for sure how long I lay injured on the stockroom floor, but I do know that eventually the paramedics were called. They found me completely unresponsive and still unconscious. Because of my condition they quickly assessed that I would require specialized treatment and they called in the helicopter to transport me to a trauma center an hour away. My fiancé, TW Walker, was called and they frantically told him that I had been seriously injured and that it was very bad. They advised him to get to the hospital as soon as possible.

Upon awakening, the first thing that I realized was that I had a death grip on the side of the stretcher. The whole room was spinning like some sort of carnival ride. My head felt like it was being crushed in a vice and there was an ear-piercing ring in my head. I could barely see and could make out only blurry images because my eyes were tiny slits from the blinding light in the room. There were thundering loud sounds all around me. It sounded like someone turned the volume up to full blast in my ears. My skin was on fire and I had searing pain shooting all over my body.

As I struggled to sit up and make sense out of this, I made a terrifying discovery…I couldn't move my legs. I learned later that I had suffered a traumatic brain injury and the blows to my head would affect the functioning of my entire body from then on. I couldn't feel my legs or move them without physically picking them up with special straps like lead weights. I couldn't even sit up because the dizziness and disorientation made me feel ill. My words came out all garbled and slurred. I couldn't recall details, or follow a conversation.

It was then that I knew the only person that was going to be totally responsible for my healing was me and I made a choice to begin to work on building my "Mind Movie". I was attempting to use my brain to heal myself but that was the very thing that had been so deeply affected. As much of a challenge as it was, I knew it would be an essential asset to my recovery. However, I was having difficulty building my movie because my brain wasn't cooperating. My fiancé TW never left my side and kept encouraging me by saying to me over and over again that everything was going to be alright. He told me that he believed in me and knew that one day I would get up and walk again. I was literally feeling like I had been beaten all over my body. TW and I joked about feeling like I had been in the ring with Mike Tyson.

Then it hit me…THAT WAS IT! *ROCKY*! It was one of my all time favorite movies! I don't know of a person who doesn't want to jump to their feet when they hear the first few bars of the Rocky theme song *Gonna Fly Now*. I worked hard for the next month on my therapy and playing my "mind movie" because at that point I wanted more than anything to go home. Warned that I would most likely never be completely free of the vast array of symptoms I suffered, still unable to walk, or care for myself, I was finally released to the full time care of TW. I was still unable to do anything on my own. He would have to bathe me, dress me, feed me, take me to the bathroom and manage all of my medications and therapy, all while trying to run his business.

Then I was dealt another devastating blow. One week after being released from my month stay in the rehabilitation hospital, on the way home from a doctor's appointment, TW and I were involved in a 40 mph collision with a reckless and impaired driver. My side of the vehicle took the brunt of the impact. I was startled awake with the impact and the airbag exploding in my face. My sunglasses were pushed into my eyes and my head was bouncing around. I began choking on the white chemical from the airbag and couldn't breathe. I had no escape because I couldn't walk.

Unbelievably, still in the infancy of my recovery, I sustained a second traumatic brain injury as my air bag deployed and sent my head into the passenger window. In my condition I was lucky to be alive. Many people die after sustaining a subsequent brain injury while the brain is already damaged. In the emergency room they determined that not only had I lost all the headway I had made during my rehabilitation, but now I had a host of new injuries.

The most serious of the injuries was a second brain injury, but as we would discover later: I had trauma cataracts that would threaten the complete loss of vision in my left eye. As if that weren't enough adversity to handle, as a result of the car accident: TW was now also seriously injured. He sustained a broken foot and a severe back injury that would later require several surgeries.

The weeks after the car accident were some of the darkest days we have ever faced. The negativity of both of our physical injuries and life circumstances had knocked the wind out of us...as if it even hurt to breathe. Our life was full of doctor visits, piles of bills, pain and frustration. Still, I choose to keep on with my "mind movie" and "Don't Give Up, Get Up" mantra. One day shortly after the car accident, TW said he had an idea. He told me that he had an inspiration for a new "mind movie". He said that we needed to create our wedding movie and officially set our wedding date. At first I was completely against it. I can even admit to being really angry that he would even suggest such a thing! I told TW we would have to be crazy to set the date!

Wheeling down the aisle in a wheelchair in pain, trying to recite garbled words and the great possibility losing track of what I was doing and making a complete fool out of myself was definitely not what I had in mind for our wedding. I will never forget TW, gentling taking hold of the armrests of my wheelchair, pulling me close to him and looking me directly in the eye saying in his usual joking manner, "You are going to be Mrs. Walker, so it's kind of important for you get up and get yourself WALKing again quickly. You will walk down that aisle by yourself."

Always great at making me laugh, but understanding the seriousness behind the joke, I looked right back into his eyes and it was as if my heart was the one who responded by saying "I believe it". I concentrated many times a day on playing my "mind movie" of my barefoot beach wedding where I would hear over and over "Don't Give Up, Get Up", among the splashing of the waves. I would feel the sand between my toes and the breeze on my face as I imagined myself walking down the aisle by myself. I am proud to say that on April 14, 2012, seven months after sustaining my second brain injury, TW and I were married in a beautiful barefoot beach wedding ceremony. Indeed, I did walk down the aisle by myself…just as I had heard and seen in my "mind movie" thousands of times before. When you get knocked down like we did, remember Don't Give Up, Get Up!

The legendary Zig Ziglar once said, "You can have everything in life you want, if you just help enough other people get what they want." What I hope to give you by reading this story is a new perspective with which to view challenges in your life and the tools to overcome them. It is my mission to show people how to get up and take the first step (which is always the hardest), and to go from feeling HELPless in a challenging situation to feeling HELPful. What I personally hope to get out of sharing this story with you is to become more HELPful to people on a global scale. ■

Heather O'Brien Walker

Heather O'Brien Walker was a quiet, shy Midwestern girl. However, having a family lineage of educators, diplomats and Pulitzer Prize winning journalists as role models, she learned early on that perseverance and goal achievement were paramount to success. One of her first positions was as a Franklin Covey business coach. She then advanced into a career as a trainer for the world's leading cosmetic companies. She then lent her talents to commercials and various films. The highlight of her career was being personal assistant to Hollywood actress, Demi Moore, then wife of Bruce Willis. Now, as an inspirational author, coach and speaker, she shares lessons from her experiences of overcoming adversity in the book "Don't Give Up, Get Up!" and of her unique H.E.L.P philosophy. Learn all about her life in Hollywood and living abroad, but also her heart wrenching experience of suffering two traumatic brain injuries in less than 40 days. With the privilege of walking, talking and caring for herself taken away from her temporarily, Heather shares how she fought through multiple adversities to achieve the goal of walking down the aisle to marry the man of her dreams.

Heather O'Brien Walker
HeatherOBrienWalker.com
HelpfulSpeaker.com
877-373-2723

19

My Responsibility: Inspire. Serve. Grow.

By Kimberly O'Neil

"Service to others is a part of life and involvement is not an option."

— Kimberly O'Neil

Being of service to others has been a part of my life for years. I cannot remember a time when I made decisions without thinking about how my words or actions impacted others. Equally as important has been my goal to inspire people to do more and be better than they were the day before.

Subconsciously, I have worked to inspire and serve others, while using those experiences to impact my own growth. My goal of helping others has inspired me to also want to do better and be more. It's been a cyclical process. Without a plan or understanding any part of the process, I knew early on that this was the way I was supposed to live my life. The journey, however, to living my life this way unfolded in a way that I did not see coming.

You often hear people openly say that they did not ask to be a role model and/or they choose not to accept the level of influence that they have on others. People tend to watch and emulate those things that have inspired them. In essence, some are not willing to accept that responsibility, while others may not realize the impact that their words and actions have. We absolutely have to live for ourselves, but I do not think we can fully reject the responsibility that impacts others.

My responsibility to others is rooted in my understanding that the many talents I have been given are not mine to keep. I have always known that my talents were a gift that I was to use to bring out the talents within others. What good are my gifts if I don't use them to multiply the talents in others? It seems simple enough and in the most obvious situations it works similar to my interpretation of the Parable of *Matthew 25: 14-30* in the Bible. But when you have been given talents that you don't recognize, the journey to multiplying is not necessarily a fairy tale.

Hollywood could not have written a better story for my life than my professional journey over the last 25 years. Father time has provided me with many experiences that have left many questioning, including myself, how it has unfolded like it has. From getting a team leadership position as a teenager just a few weeks after beginning my first job through a professional career that has led to my appointments as a senior executive in the government and nonprofit areas, I have been truly blessed. Unfortunately it has taken me almost the entire 25 years to recognize the value that each leg has played during the journey. Not each step was progress towards a better destination. Some were moves that caused me to reverse or even halt without warning. But nonetheless, it is a journey that I am proud of.

Shortly after my 31th birthday, I began questioning why I had been fortunate enough to be positioned as I had been professionally. I had worked for several mayors throughout the country, had two graduate degrees and had received designation as a Certified Public Manager. I had also been recruited into my dream career, later realizing that I was the youngest African American female appointed as a city manager in the United States. What an honor. Rarely taking time to celebrate or recognize the magnitude of the achievements, my life over the years has been full of major accomplishments. When I do sit back and think about them, what I first recognize is not the titles, graduate degrees or the certifications that I have held. What I think about is the gratitude that I have for the supporters—family, colleagues, mentors and staff that have contributed to my success. Without their contributions, my made for TV script would surely not be worthy of any major celebrations. While I have done the work, the support and assistance in preparation has been invaluable because of their investment in me. As I progressed in my career, my span of control increased to include leading teams of line staff as well as other senior executives. Without a doubt, I have been blessed with opportunity. Favor has been on my side. But the journey has not been without challenges, doubts and fears. I am a perfectionist. But I am equally a fierce competitor, but not one that brags on achievements. My harshest competition is the opponent who stares back at me through the mirror each day. I compete with myself to be better than I was the day before.

With all of that work, I began to grow weary. I relocated to Texas and began working in an extremely challenging work environment. Leadership was not trained or prepared for the organizational tasks. The day to day environment was always chaotic. No work environment is perfect, but this was toxic. I was not used to being surrounded by leaders who were committed to their own personal agendas first, and serving others as time permitted. I witnessed the morale and spirit of employees being broken. It was truly a dark period where I could not see the light coming any time in the future. Mentally, physically and emotionally I was exhausted. Visits to the doctors, frequent trips to the emergency room, sleeping pills and chest pains became part of my norm for over 3 years due to the stress from the work environment. I wore a mask to maintain my responsibility to others but behind the mask I was crumbling. Through all of my work with others, I reiterated over and over how important it was to understand the value of what you contributed to any environment. When you could no longer contribute, it was time for change. For the first time, I was not leading based on experience or advice. I was not growing through my own goals of inspiring and serving others to make a better me.

Shortly after my 38th birthday, I finally realized that all of these professional achievements lacked one thing—passion. I served in capacities that many dream of and I was great at what I did. But I was not passionate about the majority of it. Far from retirement age, I mentally retired. I realized that I stayed in positions longer than I wanted to usually because of my connection to my subordinate staff. Helping others to achieve their goals and dream bigger and better than their imagination fuels me—it is my passion. It is part of my life's work and the legacy I hope to be remembered for. But more importantly, it is my responsibility.

In September 2010, I woke up and realized that my gas tank had finally reached empty. Years of working 10-16 hour days, not taking vacations and often working alongside those who did not understand their responsibility in being a servant leader had taken its toll on me. Add to that the type of environment I was in daily, and I knew that a change had to come soon. While my energy each day was fueled by being better than the day before and helping others along the way, my soul had reached its limit. I could no longer stay in work environments that did not allow me to serve effectively. It was counterproductive. After four hours of sitting in absolute silence and meditating, I made the decision to walk away from it all. There was no plan. There was no magnificent future goal. All that was left was the professional reputation of a servant leader who needed to rest. Surely this wasn't how my Hollywood script was going to end. Little did I know that the sequel had already begun.

After submitting my 90-day resignation notice, my immediate subordinates and those of my colleagues filled my office daily. There were tears and sadness. There were pleas for me to stay. For the first time in years, I had fully come to understand my influence and had begun to feel like I was abandoning my responsibilities. I knew that my future was going to be greater than my past but for the first time in my life I did not feel like my steps were ordered.

The only thing that I knew for sure was that my life was going to be dedicated to helping others to live life with purpose.

The 90 days had passed and January 1, 2011 was the day it all started over. Off of payroll and free of day-to-day responsibilities, my heart was still heavy thinking of the people that I left behind. But I made a commitment that it was time for me to move on, yet life does not always move according to your plans. While I was not on site physically, communication with those that listened to my words and paid attention to my actions did not cease. My influence and my responsibility were far from over.

I often encouraged staff and mentors over the years to imagine life on another level. It was important for them to be cognizant of those things that inspired and fueled them. For the first time in a long time, I had to practice what I had been preaching. What I realized is that I no longer wanted to work in the capacity that I was accustomed to. I no longer wanted restrictions in what I could accomplish and how I could impact others. If I had a choice, I no longer wanted to work around others who were fueled by ego and not by service. So I opted to do more, be better and stay committed to my responsibilities in serving others while multiplying my talents within them. I chose to use January 1, 2011 as a new beginning. Decades of experience were starting to come full circle and I decided to become a full-time entrepreneur. I wanted to write my own rules and walk in the purpose that I know I was placed on earth to do. For the first time, I was free to be creative and to serve as I saw fit. But one thing remained constant—my responsibility to others.

Now in my fourth decade on earth, life has truly begun. When I look back at my accomplishments, the struggles, the sleepless nights, the missed vacations and the personal sacrifices, I look forward and recognize opportunity. But I also look at the present and what's on either side of me. I see executives, entrepreneurs and students who reach out to me and let me know how I have inspired them to be more. You see, my success is not just in my professional and educational achievements. It is also in the journeys that others have taken along the way.

We all should be willing to accept the responsibility. We need to inspire others to be the best that they can be by influencing those that are watching us. We should serve others where they may need help along the way by using our talents to assist them. It is also important to grow from the experiences of inspiring and serving others. What we do for others is a reflection of our life's work and legacy.

My life is pretty clear right now. The Hollywood sequel is being written and I am quite sure that there will be numerous iterations along the way. A great professional career full of sacrifice was well worth it because I am now writing the script. My story will end with several spinoffs showcasing the many people that I am called to serve. My life's work is to make a difference in lives. It should be part of each of our life's work Imagine what a world we could be if we all lived by three simple words—Inspire. Serve. Grow. ■

Kimberly O'Neil

Kimberly O'Neil, MPA, MA, CPM is the Chief Executive Officer of The Giving Blueprint, a company that provides philanthropic strategies to public figures and creates sustainability plans for nonprofits. A veteran government and nonprofit senior executive, she was appointed as the youngest African American woman city manager in the United States, worked in the executive offices of several mayoral administrations throughout the country, served as an adjunct college professor and was the President/Executive Director of Pro Football Hall of Famer Darrell Green's nonprofit organization, the Youth Life Foundation. Kimberly also serves as a leadership mentor, trainer and speaker.

Kimberly O'Neil, MPA, MA, CPM
Founder/CEO
The Giving Blueprint
PO Box 262574
Plano, Texas 75026
(682) 200-9546
kimberlyoneil.com
givingblueprint.com